3 DAYS TILL DAWN

By VINCE AIELLO

Published by SarEth Publishing House
SarEth Publishing House
Carlsbad, California

Cover Photography & Photo Editing © 2018 Sarah Rose Aiello
Armorer Advisor: Ethan P. Aiello

First Edition: May 2018

Printed in the United States of America

ISBN 978-0-9883413-8-8

SPHN 18-1129201706

SArEtH ™
SarEth Publishing House

Also by Vince Aiello

LEGAL DETRIMENT

THE LITIGATION GUY

LEGION'S LAWYERS

FAITH FULL

LETHAL EQUITY

*For **Fr. Michael Robinson** – A great pastor,
a great preacher, and a great teacher.*

*For **Marion & Wayne Patterson** –
Good friends, good teachers, and inspiring leaders.*

*For **Lucila Anibarro** – Our Lucy.
The inspiration for the character, Rey.*

PRAYER TO
SAINT MICHAEL THE ARCHANGEL

St. Michael the Archangel, defend us in battle.
Be our defense against the wickedness and snares of the Devil.
May God rebuke him, we humbly pray,
and do thou,
O Prince of the heavenly hosts,
by the power of God,
thrust into hell Satan,
and all the evil spirits,
who prowl about the world
seeking the ruin of souls. Amen.

-Pope Leo XIII

The way of the wicked is as **darkness**:
they know not at what they stumble.

-Proverbs 4:19

PROLOGUE

A NORTH MOLLISON AVENUE TOWNHOME
EL CAJON, CALIFORNIA

Shortly before 1:00 pm, the sun blazed mercilessly down on the El Cajon landscape. The temperature had reached 94 degrees and continued to climb. The average temperature for this time of year was 82 degrees, but the sun in El Cajon had a reputation for turning a home into a prison cell for its residents. The sun in this area had the potential to burn skin, prematurely age people, and cause heat stroke. It had the power of a venomous snake.

El Cajon is a city located in 'inland' San Diego County. Despite its geographic location, it does not share the tropical beauty of the City of San Diego. Its affordability provides most of its attractiveness. It is in a valley surrounded by mountains and its name is from a Spanish phrase meaning "the box."

The townhomes at this North Mollison Avenue location were faded yellow and three-stories tall. There was brown trim painted around the windows, but the fascia boards were dilapidated and rotting due to neglect.

On one side of the townhomes, the front doors faced either the street or an interior driveway. Each townhome had a garage on the lowest level. The backside of two rows of townhomes faced each other, creating an alley between them. It was the second garage from the southern end of one of the rows, where a flurry of activity was transpiring.

The interior of the garage was clean, but appeared depleted and barren. The walls were unfinished plasterboard and the floor was concrete with a plethora of cracks from ancient settlement.

In the center of the garage, five men sat on folding chairs. All were between the ages of twenty and thirty, clean-shaven, short, neatly-cut hair, wearing dress slacks, white shirts, and muted-color ties. No one spoke a word as they all looked forward appearing somewhat dazed, but still cognizant of their surroundings and focused on their leader.

The door from the townhome opened and a large, heavyset man entered. He was 61 years old, 275 pounds, with a finely-trimmed salt and pepper beard and receding hairline. He also wore dress slacks with a blue, long-sleeve button shirt, and a sweater vest. His visage was stern: no nonsense and his gait reflected prestige and power. There was no chair for him, but he had no interest in sitting. He was the author and architect of the meeting. He was in charge.

As he spoke, he would outstretch his arms, palms down, fingers spread, to amplify his control of the men through body language.

"Gentlemen," he announced in his careful Middle Eastern accent as he surveyed the men, "I must admit that I am envious of you and what you are about to undertake. Before the end of this day, you will all be in paradise. Greeted by both Muhammad and Allah, given a kiss on the cheek, and praised for your service."

None of the men reacted. They simply looked forward.

"You men know my name. Abdul Muhsi. Does anyone know what my name means?"

The room was silent. No one was willing to respond.

"It means 'Servant of the Reckoner.' That is exactly what you and I are today. A force of nature that cannot be stopped. A comeuppance to a great super power and a massive slaughter to a virulent pest.

"We are forced to engage in this jihad, because our enemy has enlisted the United States as their enforcer. They stand behind the United States and laugh at us like we were impotent fools. Their reputation is to get someone else to do their dirty work. It is time to punish the bully for their choices.

"We are going to bring terror to an area thought to be safe. America must learn that as long as they back this scourge, they will pay the price in blood. And our enemies must learn that there is a target on their backs and we will not rest until their existence is obliterated from the face of the earth.

"The goal of today's mission is volume. Both in number and in message – to resonate throughout the world. According to my calculations, the casualty list should exceed one thousand. And the history books, written by our historians, will record your names in awe and glory.

"Our goal is simple: to eradicate the world of the malignant and pernicious blight that vexes our very existence. I am speaking of the cancer known as the vile, common, gutter Jew."

Several of the men nodded their heads in agreement with his caustic diatribe. The others were hoping that the day would just end soon.

Day 1
TUESDAY

CHAPTER 1

2 DAYS EARLIER

Oceanside, California is the northernmost city in the County of San Diego. It is also the third largest city with a population of nearly 170,000 people. The city has a large military influence as it is located just south of the Camp Pendleton Marine Corps base.

On the corner of South Coast Highway and West Topeka Avenue sits the Dolphin Hotel. Built in 1927, the two-story structure, situated in the downtown area and just blocks from the ocean, had fallen into decline in recent years. Its twenty-seven rooms mostly served as studio apartments to a transient population. It was the first hotel in the area to have a bathroom in every room. In the 1930s and 40s, the hotel boasted glitz and allure, but now it was more of a flophouse, serving the needs of those just barely making it to the poverty line.

The interior of the lobby was resplendent with mahogany furniture. It featured a public telephone from ninety years earlier, sited inside a small chamber, like a coffin, that allowed the user to close the bi-fold door once inside. The reception desk was plain and simple and behind it sat mail slots for each room to allow a tenant to pick up their mail.

All the rooms ran off a main hallway and the view from the rooms was either a street or an alley.

At 7:45 am this day, Jack Vance emerged from Apartment 203 and was putting on his blue windbreaker as he was exiting. Jack was 53 years old, six feet tall with a thirty-four inch waist. He was clean-shaven with a full head of salt and pepper hair. His clothes were part of a uniform. His windbreaker revealed his first name over one breast pocket and the Buick automobile logo over the other.

Jack moved at a steady pace, down the hallway to Apartment 212, and he rapped his fist swiftly against the door.

"Rey, you ready?" he asked through the door.

"I'm coming," responded a voice.

The door opened and there stood Rey. She was 89 years old, 5 feet 4 inches tall, spry and sturdy. Her smile beamed and it was infectious. She wore a grey wool skirt, white button shirt and a blue knit sweater. The clothes were worn, but not threadbare. They were used frequently, but always looked fresh and fit her perfectly. Her outfit was accented with a pill box hat that matched her skirt and had a small piece of French veil attached to it.

"I'm ready," she announced. "I've got a new friend I just met yesterday. Can we give her a ride?"

"Sure. Is she close by?" Jack wondered.

"Right next door."

Rey scurried to Apartment 214 and, while still in motion, began to speak.

"Sophie, you ready?"

"Yeah, I'm ready," came a voice as the door opened.

Sophie Jansen was 24 years old with a waif-like frame and quite similar in size to Rey. She wore a light purple bohemian top with three-quarter length sleeves, a green and light brown knit sweater, and blue Levi's 505 jeans. She had a cuteness to her face that had no trace of makeup. Her expression was somber and dour with a smile that was forced.

"Sophie, this is Jack," Rey exclaimed.

"Nice to meet you," Sophie said. "Thank you for the ride."

"No problem," Jack answered. "Welcome to the Dolphin. If you need anything, just ask Rey or me."

"Thanks, I really appreciate it." A smile finally filled her face. "If you guys need your clothes washed, I work at the Laundromat Lounge, just down the street. I can do them for you."

"Rey," Jack announced. "I think today is our lucky day."

"Praise be to God!" Rey proudly proclaimed.

That comment brought a smile to all of them.

"Let's get going," Jack declared and swung his head toward the front of the building.

Both ladies followed Jack down the hallway to the stairs and out the front door to Coast Highway. Jack was able to park on the street, so his black Honda Accord sat within a few feet of the Hotel's entrance door.

Rey sat in the passenger seat and Sophie was right behind her. Jack opened the doors for both ladies and closed them after they were in. He moved hastily to the driver's seat and their journey was underway.

Their expedition took less than five minutes, including parking, and they arrived at St. Mary, Star of the Sea Church, located on Pier View Way.

The chapel for this church was built in 1893 and the church itself was completed in 1927. Located on the east side of the church was a Memorial Wall with a grotto honoring Saint Juan Diego, to whom the Blessed Virgin Mary appeared as Our Lady of Guadalupe.

Rey, Jack, and Sophie entered the church and Sophie gazed upon it in wonder. It had a high ceiling, white, painted walls, and twenty rows of pews. Rey entered a pew that was in the second row from the back of the church. Rey and Sophie knelt on a kneeler to commence praying, while Jack opted to sit.

Father Gerardo Fernandez began the service and moved at an energetic pace. The readings and blessings came and went. Then it was time for the portion of the Mass where bread and wine are consecrated and shared. Row by row, the parishioners advanced to the altar to receive Holy Communion. Sophie, Jack, and Rey all exited the pew, but only Rey proceeded to the altar. Jack and Sophie regained their seats and knelt down.

Jack looked forward without focus, lost in thought. Sophie looked down and rested her forehead on her clasped hands. A single tear rolled down her cheek. Both had a reason for not taking communion and at this moment, by happenstance, both had the same thought: Are there sins that God won't forgive?

CHAPTER 2

Ten blocks south of the Dolphin Hotel and one block to the east, sat the Agua Dulce Apartments. The name was written in large, cursive letters on the street side of the building. The two-story structure was in extreme disrepair and its residents consisted of mainly Section 8 housing participants. Created by the U.S. Department of Housing and Urban Development, the Section 8 program allows local public housing agencies to issue vouchers for housing to economically-challenged individuals and families.

Peddlers of marijuana and crack cocaine would always be able to find a customer here as most residents simply wanted to escape their lives, if only for a brief moment.

Rory Dahl lived in Unit 6, the end unit on the first floor. Rory was 26 years old, a college dropout, who was dishonorably discharged from the Marines for striking a commanding officer. He was 5 feet 10 inches tall, 194 pounds, with black, thinning curly hair. He always wore cargo shorts and a variety of ratty, scruffy t-shirts. Rory was now receiving disability checks after he fell off a first floor scaffold while working for a local construction company.

Inside of Unit 6, dust was seen on all the 1950s furniture, as well as strewn pizza boxes and newspapers. Cockroaches scurried about boldly, without fear of extermination, while the television blasted the *CNN Headline News*.

Rory stood in the bathroom facing the sink and spat out foamy toothpaste after completing the brushing of his teeth. He then picked up a large bottle of Listerine, took a swig, gargled it back, and spit it out. He picked up a towel, gave it a quick sniff, and then wiped his mouth. He threw the towel to the floor and proceeded to the living room/kitchen.

On the kitchen counter sat a five gallon fish tank with two large goldfish swimming with carefree wonder. Rory picked up a package of TetraFin Flakes, situated at the end of the counter, opposite the fish tank. He returned to the fish tank and began to sprinkle the flakes.

"Good morning, Mr. Fish, Good morning Mrs. Fish," he announced with muted bravado. "How is everyone today?"

Rory tapped the fish food package several times and stopped.

"I saw on the news last night that these guys broke into a house and poured a whole bottle of tequila into the fish tank. Killed all the fish. What kind of an animal does that?"

Rory then squatted down slightly to survey the bottom of the fish tank. There were small ceramic figures of a deep sea diver, a chest of treasure, a small house, and an octopus.

"What did you think of my new girlfriend?" he inquired, then paused. "What do you think, Mr. Fish? Mrs. Fish? Do you think she could be the one? Do you think she could learn to love me?"

He slowly stood as he continued to speak.

"I find my life boring. What I want is an off-the-shelf wife. I want to be able to use her whenever and however I want and then simply put her on a shelf when I'm done. I don't want to be bothered by her and when I'm done with her, I'll simply find another."

Rory moved to his worn, black backpack and wrenched it from the floor. He threw it over his shoulder and made a beeline to the front door when he suddenly stopped. He turned back and walked over to the closet.

The closet door had three deadbolts on it. They were commercial strength with reinforced steel. Rory slid each of the deadbolts to the open position and opened the door. As light flooded the closet, clothes could be seen hanging inside the door way. He reached his arm in and swept back the clothes from right to left.

On the right side of the closet, a naked girl, named Carol Ann Zelinsky, was handcuffed with the handcuffs going over the metal pole that held up the clothes. Her body weight dangled from the handcuffs. Duct tape circled her face around her mouth and her head drooped forward without strength. She slowly raised her head with passive energy. Both eyes were blackened and dried blood could be seen under her nose.

Rory stared at her for a moment. On the closet walls were sound-canceling acoustic panels and it housed a bucket for her toilet needs.

"I'm gonna go get you something to eat." He then took a moment to peruse her. "Don't worry. You will learn to love me."

Rory suddenly disappeared from the closet as darkness returned and Carol Ann heard the three deadbolts move to the locked position. She began to pray that someone would come to save her.

CHAPTER 3

After church, Jack dropped off Rey at the Dolphin Hotel and Sophie at the Laundromat Lounge. He then proceeded directly to his work located in Carlsbad. Carlsbad is the city located immediately south of Oceanside. It has a collection of car dealerships all in one location with the name, Car Country Carlsbad. It consists of two streets that are lined with nearly every brand of car dealership, including Porsche, Mercedes, and Jaguar.

Even though there were acres and acres of new and used cars for sale or lease, employees were forced to park on the street. It was always something of a crapshoot, but Jack viewed it as a game. If he found a convenient parking space, he would have a good day. If not, he expected the day to go from bad to worse.

Jack found a parking space approximately one and one-half blocks from Thunderbar Buick, his employer. Jack had worked there for the past four years as a customer shuttle driver. People would drop off their cars as early as 6:30 am and the dealership provided them with a ride anywhere within a ten mile radius.

As Jack proceeded to his work space area, he shared his customary salutations with a handful of employees. His manager,

Bill Godfrey, wanted to say a little more than just 'Hello' to him this morning.

"Morning, Bill," Jack blurted out in passing.

"Hey, Jack. You got a minute?"

"Yeah," Jack acknowledged. "What's going on?"

"You've only got one rider this morning. The guy lives out in El Cajon. He bought his Buick Roadmaster here in 1996 and we've done the service on it ever since. We promised him when he bought the car, we'd get him back to El Cajon. He's been here since about 6:45. So, take care of it."

"El Cajon? That's gotta be at least forty miles. With traffic, it'll take me all morning."

"Whatever it is, it is. We'll be here when you get back."

Bill handed Jack a transport sheet and gave him a quick slap on the shoulder.

Jack perused the transport sheet. It contained information on the customer, a description of the car, and the car's license plate number. The customer's name was Abdul "Al" Muhsi.

He then headed to the back of the dealership where the customer service shuttle vehicles were parked. Jack selected a late-model Buick Envision sport utility vehicle. He drove it to the customer service entrance, but noticed the SUV was low on gas. Jack decided to worry about this after he located his passenger.

The customer service lounge for the dealership was adjacent to the customer service attendant's area. Jack entered and surveyed those waiting for a ride.

"Mr. Muhsi?" Jack announced.

"Right here, my friend."

Abdul Muhsi was reading the local paper and perked up when he heard his named called. He immediately removed his reading glasses and placed them in the pocket of his grey windbreaker.   He also wore black Dockers pants with black Florsheim loafers.

Jack locked eyes with him and, for a nanosecond, Abdul's face appeared to him like an x-ray. The eyes were hollow and black. His teeth could be seen down to the roots. It gave Jack a terrifying chill. Within that second, the image was gone.

Abdul walked over to Jack. Jack began to speak as he approached.

"I'm ready to go," he advised. "I need gas. We can get it on the way, if that's okay with you."

"No problem, my friend," Abdul replied with his Middle Eastern accent and a wide smile.

"Let's go," Jack told him and they made their way to the SUV.

Once inside the vehicle, Jack put Abdul's address into the onboard navigation system. Their journey had begun.

They traveled down Paseo Del Norte, the street where the dealership was located.

"How's the weather out in El Cajon these days?" Jack inquired.

"Hot."

"Do you have to keep the air conditioning on all the time?"

"Yes. Otherwise, it is unbearable."

"Do you work in El Cajon?" Jack wondered.

"I'm a professor of Middle Eastern history at the community college. I'm semi-retired."

"That's nice," Jack retorted as his mind raced for the next harmless question. But Abdul decided to interject one.

"Do you speak Farsi, my friend?"

Farsi is a Middle Eastern language spoken in various parts of Iran and Iraq.

"No," Jack said assuredly. "Only English."

"Understood, my friend. If you will excuse me, I'm going to make a call."

"Go ahead."

Abdul dialed a number on his Smartphone and placed it on speaker. Within three rings, it was answered. The conversation began, but sounded like garbled noise to Jack. Shortly after it began, it turned to English for just a few sentences.

"Don't worry if you don't have one. It can't be intercepted. There's no backdoor trace. And there's no record of the call," Abdul advised with serious importance. The conversation returned to garbled noise.

Jack found those few sentences to be very curious and troubling. As he continued to drive, he removed his Smartphone from his inside breast pocket. He opened the application for the voice recorder and began to record the conversation.

As the conversation proceeded, Jack would catch an occasional glimpse of Abdul in his rearview mirror. The wheels in Jack's mind were smoking. He had seen a face with an x-ray image, like he had seen on Abdul, once before. It was the moment before Jack's life was totally destroyed.

CHAPTER 4

Inside the North Mollison Avenue townhome of Abdul Muhsi, Abdul prepared for the arrival of guests. He reviewed a biography sheet of each of the attendees and also the background check that was conducted for each individual.

The doorbell rang and Abdul scurried to answer it. He opened the door and there stood Rafid Nasif, 29 years old, slender build, with black, thick hair, and dark skin. Abdul had a look of surprise on his face. He immediately uttered an angry comment to him in Farsi. Rafid looked at him with puzzled wonder.

"Get in here," Abdul demanded.

Rafid briskly entered.

"Didn't I tell you to use the keypad on the overhead door downstairs to get in here? What if the FBI was watching that door?"

"Your keypad is not working. The rest of the men are waiting down there," Rafid answered.

"You have not been studying your Farsi. What are you going to tell Allah when he asks you why you only speak the language of the pig?"

Rafid gazed at Abdul.

"Follow me," Abdul ordered and they proceeded down to the garage area.

Abdul opened the overhead door and five men entered. All had the same physical size and appearance as Rafid.

"Gentlemen," Abdul told them, "we are going to talk upstairs for a while, then move back down here. None of you will leave here before the appointed time. For the next two nights you will sleep on the floor upstairs. I will go out for food and bring it back."

"Is your wife here?" one of the men inquired.

"No. She is back home visiting family. Let us proceed."

Abdul climbed the staircase followed by the six men and directed them to each take a seat at his dining room table. Once seated, Abdul stood at the head of the table preparing for a sermon.

"*Allah Akbar*," Abdul began. "What does it mean?"

"God is greater," one of the men quickly spoke up.

"Greater than what?" Abdul inquired.

"Greater than you and I," the same man answered.

"Allah is greater than anything that can be comprehended. That is why, to serve him, is the greatest gift you can pay to him. The greatest thing that you can give to Allah on this earth is your life. When you do it in his name, for his glory, and to extinguish an enemy, this is the greatest praise possible. And in thanksgiving to you, you will spend eternity in paradise, living like devoted sons, with any dream or desire fulfilled."

Abdul gazed around the table.

"Do you have any questions?"

The room was silent. Some of the men shook their head slightly in a negative response.

"You, gentlemen, have seen firsthand the financial inequity of this country. They don't want us here because we are willing to work for success. No one gives it to us and when we achieve it, they look for ways to take it away from us. And who seeks to stop us? I know, and I believe you know."

Abdul again surveyed the room.

"Who was the greatest president of the United States?" He paused. "I want answers."

"Washington," one of the men blurted out.

"Lincoln," said another.

"It was Harry S. Truman," Abdul told them. "During World War II, some people wondered why Truman did not do anything to stop Hitler's Final Solution or save the Jews. Truman put the answer in his diary in 1947. He wrote, and I quote, 'The Jews, I find, are very, very selfish.' He went on to say, 'They care not how many Estonians, Latvians, Finns, Poles, Yugoslavs or Greeks get murdered or mistreated as Displaced Persons as long as the Jews get special treatment. Yet when they have power, physical, financial or political, neither Hitler nor Stalin has anything on them for cruelty or mistreatment to the underdog.

"Gentlemen," Abdul continued, "this is called 'tacit acceptance' by Truman of Hitler's action. It is approval based on non-action. Truman obviously recognized the scourge and knew what had to be done."

Abdul gave one final glance around the table.

"I want you to think about what we have discussed. I will go get us something to eat. Rafid, you will be in charge. On the workbench in the garage is a metal detector. Check all the men. Make sure none of them have a recording device or telephone. We'll continue our discussions when I return."

"May we watch television?" one of the men asked.

"No. It is controlled by Jews in New York. I suggest prayer."

Abdul left the room. The men looked around at each other, but none of them started a conversation. They all stood from the table in unison and Rafid led them to the basement.

The plan had commenced.

CHAPTER 5

On the way back to Thunderbar Buick, Jack could focus on nothing but his passenger's conversation. Worrying about calls being intercepted, a backdoor trace, and no record of the call seemed terribly suspicious. Jack knew that a backdoor trace would allow a hacker to access information stealthily from a phone.

What bothered Jack the most, but what he did not want to focus on, was the image of Abdul's face like an x-ray that appeared for a brief moment. He had seen it once before and he feared it.

As he drove, he made a phone call to an old friend. It was answered on the second ring.

"Is this who I think it is?" the voice answered with pumped-up enthusiasm.

"What's going on, Deke?" Jack answered.

Deacon Cykes was a friend of Jack's for the past twenty-five years. Deke was a Cause and Origin Specialist with the City of San Diego Fire Department for twenty years before starting a third career as a meat cutter in a local Vons supermarket. But it was Deke's first career that Jack was interested in for this phone call.

"Trying to stay above the ground my friend, and you?"

"Just working. How's the family?"

"They're good. My wife and I are finally empty nesters and loving every minute of it."

"Did your youngest son move out?"

"No. We sold the house and moved to a smaller one."

"Genius."

"It was time. You doing anything social?"

"No."

"Still up in that fleabag hotel?"

"Yeah, but it's all right."

"You gotta walk out of that prison, Jack. Life is for the living," Deke admonished.

"You're right. Listen, I wanted to ask you for a favor."

"Sure. What is it?"

"You still got friends in the Company?"

The Company that Jack was referring to was the CIA.

"I think there are a couple of my students still roaming around there."

"I want to send you a recording that I just made during one of my rides. Get someone to listen to it and let me know what they think."

"Did your rider know they were being recorded? Otherwise, there are some legal problems."

"I don't know if it's nothing or something big. I just want to find out."

"All right, send it to me. I'll see what I can do."

"Can you put a rush on it?" Jack asked.

"You want breakfast in bed, too?" Deke quipped. "You owe me a coffee."

"Done," Jack responded quickly.

"And donuts."

"All right. Adios, my friend,"

"Toodles." With that, the call ended.

When Jack reached the dealership, he took a picture of the transport sheet that had Abdul Muhsi's contact information. He sent that, along with a copy of the conversation recording, to Deke.

Jack had a nagging suspicion that the conversation was not innocent. He awaited Deke's confirmation.

CHAPTER 6

The Laundromat Lounge featured three rows of twenty, high-capacity washing machines, and one double-decker row of industrial clothes dryers. There was also a payphone, a Coke machine, and a vending machine that sold small packages of soap, bleach, and dryer sheets. In addition, there was a bill-changing machine that would provide quarters and smaller coins to operate the washers and dryers.

Sophie was busy assisting a customer, whose dryer was shaking so hard, it appeared as if it was going to break apart. Sophie stopped the machine and removed the overstuffed load of sheets and blankets.

"*Demasiado,* (Too much,)" she told the Mexican patron. "You have to take them apart. Otherwise, they bind up and get too heavy for the machine."

As she spoke, Sophie used hand gestures in an attempt to amplify the message that she was trying to impart. The woman simply smiled and shook her head affirmatively. Sophie then handed her nine quarters.

While Sophie dealt with the customer, Rory entered the laundromat. He moved swiftly to the dollar changing machine and planned to exchange three dollar bills for quarters. His face had a scowl as if he was impatient to wait for the machine to operate. After he received change for the first dollar, he noticed Sophie.

"Excuse me," he called out to her in an attempt to secure her attention.

"Yes?" she asked wondering what might be the problem.

"The machine's not taking my dollars. You want to try it?"

Sophie approached Rory and he reached out to hand her a dollar. She went up to the machine. It took the dollar and spit out four quarters. She scooped up the quarters and dropped them into Rory's palm.

"You must have the magic touch," Rory told her with a somewhat awkward gaze.

"The machine can be temperamental," she advised.

"My name's Rory."

"Hi, Rory."

"What's your name?"

"Sophie."

"You live around here?"

"Not too far."

"I've been looking for a place. I wonder if you have a recommendation."

"Sorry, I don't. I need to get back to my Fluff & Fold."

"What's Fluff & Fold?" Rory inquired.

"You can drop off your dirty clothes, then we wash them, dry them, and fold them for you."

"Like dry cleaning?"

"Not quite. They use chemicals then press the clothes," Sophie answered.

"Do you iron the clothes?"

"If you fold them right when they come out of the dryer, there's no need."

"I came in to use your phone. Can't find a pay phone anymore."

"They have a lot of them at the train station across the street."

"I'm not much for crossing the street," Rory informed her.

"I'll let you get to your call," Sophie responded and immediately began to move away from him. He raised his hand as if he was going to grab her arm, but did not touch her. Sophie gave a slight startled reaction to the thought of Rory touching her.

"Would you like to go for coffee sometime?"

"Thanks, but I don't think so."

"How about an ice cream?"

"No, I'm not interested. If you need anything, just let me know. I'll be in the back."

Sophie moved hastily away from Rory. He gave off a vibe that Sophie found disturbing. She went into the back office and locked the door. For a moment, she contemplated calling nine-one-one.

Rory watched her walk away and stewed over her rejection. He knew that she wasn't going anyplace and he knew where to find her. At that moment, Rory saw an Oceanside Police car pull up and park in front of the Laundromat Lounge. He decided to leave.

In his mind, Rory now believed that Sophie was the next woman who would learn to love him.

CHAPTER 7

Around 7:00 pm that evening, Jack made it back to the Dolphin Hotel. The hotel manager, Flip Tuluke, sat behind the check-in counter reading the book, *Slaughterhouse 5*, by Kurt Vonnegut. He was focused and occasionally ran his finger across the page, so he would not lose his place. Flip was 74 years old, bald, heavyset, and always had a beaming smile. Jack could not pass him without a salutation and some small talk.

"Flip," Jack called out in an elevated voice to accommodate Flip's slight hearing loss. "What are you up to?"

Flip looked up and removed his reading glasses. He exchanged them for a pair that he used for distance vision.

"Evening, Mr. Jack. Another day at the mill?"

"You got that right," Jack answered as he approached the counter. "You busy?"

"Nah, not really. On Tuesdays, I check my lottery numbers down at the liquor store. But my numbers haven't come in for the past forty years." Flip's comment made him introspective and somber. "Tonight, I'm just reading. The light's better down here. The owner won't spring for cable TV."

"How'd you get the name, Flip?"

Flip gave him an awkward glance.

"You're old enough to remember Flip Wilson? *The Flip Wilson Show*? Thursday nights at eight o'clock. Back in the late 60s, it was the funniest show on television. My mama was proud to have a son named Flip. My dad, not so much."

"I remember," Jack said. "He used to put on a dress sometimes."

"Geraldine," Flip cut him off. "The devil made me do it."

Jack lost focus when Flip spoke his last sentence. He re-focused.

"That was a good show," Jack acknowledged. "I gotta get going. You have a good evening."

"You too, Mr. Jack."

Jack added one final comment as he started to walk away.

"I hope your lottery numbers come in."

"From your lips to God's ears," Flip proclaimed.

As Jack ascended the staircase, he could not change his focus. He was transfixed by the words, "The devil made me do it."

CHAPTER 8

Rory's hostage, Carol Ann Zelinsky, spent the day attempting to pull down the metal closet rod over which she was handcuffed. The flange that held it up had four screws and she could see that her efforts were beginning to bear fruit. Carol was able to get a little movement of the flange away from the wall. She feared that if she tore it down and Rory came home, he would beat her or kill her immediately.

Carol's arms were burning from being in an upright position for more than a day. When she wasn't trying to pull down the closet rod, she was either crying or hanging there in abject exhaustion.

Carol convinced herself that she was not going to die in this closet or this apartment. The wall to her right was shared with the next door apartment. Her anxiety turned into vitriolic rage as she started to slam her foot into one of the pieces of soundproofing material. It was glued to the wall and when she stomped on it, Carol could feel some flexibility in the wall. She gripped the closet rod with one hand for bracing and began stomping on the wall. Carol ran out of energy almost immediately. Her mouth was dry and Rory never brought her any food.

She heard a noise and feared it was Rory. She ceased her efforts and passed out from exhaustion.

At the Laundromat Lounge, Sophie helped the final customer of the day fold her clothes and began to shut off the lights. The customer was heavyset with gray hair and thick glasses. She locked the doors before undertaking any other closing activity.

Sophie walked to the front doors and scanned South Coast Highway. Daylight was fading and dusk had arrived. She turned to the customer.

"Excuse me," Sophie inquired, "are you heading north on South Coast Highway?"

"Yeah," she replied with a smile.

"Can I walk with you?"

"Sure," she responded. "I only go about four blocks."

Sophie and the woman began their trek and Sophie's concerns dissipated with each step. They said their goodbyes at Leonard Avenue. Sophie moved in haste for the next six blocks to the Dolphin Hotel. She felt relief when she opened the door and saw Flip.

Across the street from the Dolphin Hotel was the Señor Pancho Mexican Grill. It had a large parking lot, but it was not fully lit. In the darkness, and standing next to the adjoining building was Rory Dahl. He gazed at the Dolphin Hotel with vacuous emotion. His mission was successful. He now knew where Sophie lived.

CHAPTER 9

When Jack walked into his apartment at the Dolphin Hotel, the only light came from the sole window, which provided light from neon signs and moonlight. The screened window was partially opened and a breeze wafted in. Jack did not turn on any lights. His studio apartment consisted of a bed, a counter with a microwave on it, and cabinets above the counter. There was no television or telephone. The room smelled slightly musty and even in the dark, the presence of dust was evident.

Jack hung up his windbreaker and sat on the side of the bed looking out the window. The window allowed the sounds of Oceanside at night to enter – loud voices, deafening radios from passing cars, the occasional siren, and a breeze blowing off the ocean.

Jack was pensive regarding the day's events until he heard a rap on his door.

"Yeah," he called out.

"Jack," Rey said through the door, "come on over. I made some iced tea."

Jack thought it sounded like a good idea. After removing his tie and throwing it on the bed, he took a brisk jaunt to Rey's apartment. It was Jack's turn to knock on the door.

"Jack," Rey spoke up, "come on in."

Jack entered into a studio apartment filled with light, exceptionally clean, and graced with a charming hostess. Rey stood over a plate of cookies, then held the plate out to Jack.

"Try one," she offered.

"If you insist," he responded as he took one of the small circular cookies from the tray. The cookie had a hole in the center and was sprinkled with sugar. Jack put the entire cookie in his mouth.

"Rey, that's incredible," Jack pined as he reached for second one.

"That's my wine cookie. It's basically a sugar cookie with a little white wine. I was able to bake them at a friend's house."

"I am impressed."

"I'm going to send you home with a bag of them. Come on, let's sit and have some iced tea."

The iced tea was already poured, sitting in tall glasses, and loaded with ice. Rey had two chairs in her apartment at the foot of the bed, with a small table between them. Rey handed Jack a glass of tea and placed the tray of cookies between them before sitting down.

"It's not good for you to sit alone over there in the dark," Rey told him.

"I'm no stranger to darkness," he replied.

"Did you have a good day?"

"Do you want to know how I spent most of the day?" Jack asked as if he could not believe how he spent the day.

"Share."

"I had to drive a guy to El Cajon this morning. He tells me that he has to make a phone call and then asks me if I speak Farsi. You know, the Middle Eastern language?"

"Sure," Rey replied.

"He calls the person, and before he starts speaking in Farsi, the guy says a couple sentences in English, talking about the cell phone, how it can't be traced, and there's no record of the call. I just found it to be very suspicious."

Rey continued to listen attentively and smiled.

"At that point, I decided to record the phone call. I can do it off my phone. So, I recorded the phone call and I have been trying to find somebody who knows Farsi. We have a parts guy, who is from Iraq, but said he doesn't know Farsi. So, I sent it to this guy, who knows people in the government."

"Oh good, so you don't have to worry," Rey remarked in an effort to comfort him.

"Well," Jack said hanging on to the syllable, "there is one more thing. Now, you may not believe me, but I would appreciate your opinion."

"Sure, go ahead."

"When I first saw this guy, for just a moment, a flash, his face appeared to me like an x-ray. I could see his skull, his eyes were black and it was disturbing. But I had seen it once before."

"Example?"

Jack took a long sip of his iced tea and set it back on the table.

"This is quite good, by the way."

Rey smiled.

Jack continued, "I was a lawyer once. I was good at it. Five years ago, *San Diego Magazine* named me one of the top Lawyers of the Year. I put it ahead of my family, which was my first sin. I had the perfect family. A wife and two kids, a boy and a girl. I wasn't the type of father who threw the ball in the backyard, probably because I didn't have that kind of father. My son was a little awkward, but he was fascinated by the police. He wanted to be a police officer. That was his career path. He used to beg me to go to the shooting range. We did and he was good at it."

"Good at what?" Rey wondered.

"Firing a gun. So, we did that. He entered competitions and he won a few. Then he wanted a gun. And because of my guilt in neglecting him, I bought one, in my name, for him to use."

Jack was becoming more contemplative as the story progressed.

"But my son was troubled. My wife told me that he was hearing voices, but I refused to believe it. I refused to believe that a son of mine could be mentally impaired. So, I ignored it."

Jack's eyes were welling up as if he might begin to cry.

"When my son was eighteen years old, I came home one day and he was sitting in the kitchen covered in blood with the gun in his hand. When I first looked at him, I saw, for a split second, his face like an x-ray. I asked him if he was okay and what happened. He said it was an accident. The voices told me to do it. Then he said he was sorry for disappointing me. I told him to put down the gun. I would take care of it. He started to put the gun down, but. . . then. . .just," Jack burst into tears.

Rey reached over to Jack and pulled him by the arm. They both stood and Jack leaned forward to cry on her shoulder while she hugged him.

"He killed himself in front of me," Jack told her through his tears. "He also killed my wife and daughter. My whole family was gone."

After a long moment, Jack started to gain his composure and straightened up to look Rey in the face. Rey was also crying as if it had been her family. Then she reached over to the counter and grabbed a box of tissues. She offered it to Jack and they both swiped several tissues before regaining their seats.

"Is this why you don't take communion?" Rey wondered.

Jack nodded. "I killed my family."

"How are you responsible?"

"I bought the gun that was used to kill them all."

"And you think that's a sin?"

"In the law, there is a very simple test to determine liability. It's called the 'but for' test. But for me buying the gun, my family would not have been killed."

"Listen to me, Jack. Don't judge yourself by man's laws. The only one who has the right to pass definitive judgment on the works and the hearts of men is Christ the Redeemer. He acquired this right by his cross. God has given all judgment to his Son. Jesus does not come to judge, but comes to save through forgiveness of past sins. Jesus forgives the sins of the past. What are you going to do in the future? That's what Jesus is interested in. I believe that is why you have this conflict about what happened today."

"What do you think happened today?"

Rey adjusted her position in the chair.

"Have you ever studied the history of military tactics?"

"A little," Jack answered.

"Since the dawn of time there has been a battle raging, between God and his angels against Satan and his minions. It's basically good versus evil. Satan wants to destroy everything that God has created. And what he enjoys doing the most, is having God's children spread the evil. Satan believes that is a slap in the face to God. So Satan finds the weak, the feeble-minded, and plants a seed. From that day forward, a battle rages, externally and internally. The question is: How are you going to fight it?"

Rey's visage was quite stern.

"Have you ever heard the term 'Take point?" she inquired.

"Yeah. It's the leader," Jack responded.

"No. It's the person who assumes the first and most exposed position in a combat military formation. The leading soldier advancing through hostile territory. Maybe, what you are seeing is evil."

"You mean like demons?"

"It's possible. There are those in the church who believe that God has selected certain individuals to act as point men and women to assist in the battle against evil here on earth. These are the people who pose the greatest danger to Satan. They are able to disrupt his plans."

A knock at the door interrupted their conversation.

"Come on in," Rey called out.

Sophie entered with a large grocery bag filled with yarn and knitting needles.

"Hi, Rey," she blurted out, then noticed her visitor. "Oh, hi Jack."

"Come on in. We got iced tea and wine cookies," Rey told her.

As Rey poured Sophie a glass of tea, Sophie had a question.

"Jack, do you know if you can pay cash for an Uber ride?"

"You know I'm not sure. I'll find out."

"Okay. And can you also find out if you need a phone to use it. Because I don't have one."

"I never found a need for one myself," Rey chirped in.

"I don't have a bank account and if I have a social security number, I don't know what it is," Sophie shared with the group.

41

"How do you cash your paycheck?" Jack wondered.

"Mr. Capezzio, he's the owner, he pays me in cash."

"That's all right," Jack responded.

"Listen, you two," Sophie addressed them, "when you get up tomorrow, take the sheets off your bed. Wednesday is always slow, so I'm going to give them my best Fluff & Fold. And include your blankets."

"Sounds good," Jack countered. "I'll pick you up tomorrow night, so you don't have to carry everything back."

"Oh, that would be great. I had a guy come in today that really spooked me. I went in the back office and hid until he was gone. I'm able to watch the machines on a video camera."

"Be careful," Jack warned.

"Listen to him, young lady," Rey added.

"Are we ready to start knitting?" Sophie blurted out with enthusiasm.

"I'm going to call it a day," Jack announced.

"Are you sure, Jack? Tonight, I'm going to teach her how to do an incredible cable stitch."

"Rey made me this sweater."

"I'm going to pass, ladies. I'll see you in the morning."

"Don't forget your cookies," Rey interjected.

"Thanks, Rey."

Jack walked back to his room and thought about the information Rey had imparted to him. He wasn't necessarily enlightened or illuminated by it. He just thought it was interesting.

CHAPTER 10

As Sophie selected needles and yarn from her grocery bag filled with knitting supplies, Rey retrieved her bag from a small closet in the apartment.

"How was your day, honey?" Rey wondered.

"Oh, it was good except for that guy," she replied.

"What was it about him?" Rey asked as she regained her seat.

"I don't know. The way he looked at me. Then he wanted to go with me for coffee. I thought he was going to grab me, so I went back in the office. We had about a half dozen customers at the time, so I knew he wouldn't try anything."

"You have to be on your guard, sweetheart, you never know where evil may come from."

"My mother used to tell me a bible passage," Sophie told her, "that contained the word 'armor' and I always thought about a knight coming to save me when she said it."

"I'm familiar with it. It is Ephesians, Chapter 6, verses 13 through 20. It deals with the armor of God."

"I bet you have it memorized," Sophie said with certainty.

"I do."

"Would you share it with me?"

Rey was proud of Sophie's request.

"Therefore take up the full armor of God, so that when the day of evil comes, you will be able to stand your ground, and having done everything, to stand. Stand firm then, with the belt of truth fastened around your waist, with the breastplate of righteousness arrayed, and with your feet fitted with the readiness of the gospel of peace. In addition to all this, take up the shield of faith, with which you can extinguish all the flaming arrows of the evil one. And take the helmet of salvation and the sword of the Spirit, which is the word of God."

"Wow." Sophie said in awe. "That is beautiful."

Rey nodded her head in acknowledgment of the comment.

"The bible tells us what we need to do to fight evil," Rey advised. "It is up to us to follow those instructions."

"Can I tell you something?" Sophie asked sheepishly.

"Absolutely."

"I'm a twin. An identical twin. My sister's name was Trudy. Gertrude, actually. We did everything together. Dressed alike, listened to the same music, tried to screw with people's head as to who was who. But for some reason, the boys were always drawn to Trudy."

Sophie's expression turned into a pensive look. Rey repositioned her chair to face Sophie. Rey grasped both of her hands.

"There was one boy that she said was serious about her, but I told her she was too young. We were both eighteen at the time. In reality, I was jealous. Trudy said they were talking about marriage and things were happening. One day she tells me she's pregnant. Well, when the boyfriend hears that, he disappears. I tell Trudy that she can't have that baby. It'll ruin her life. The baby would be nothing more than baggage. There was so much that she and I had planned to do."

"I think I know what you are going to tell me," Rey conveyed.

"No, you don't," Sophie relayed with certainty. Her voice began a slight tremble.

"I told her that she had to get an abortion. I told her that I would help her pay for it. I told her that I would make the appointment and go with her. But Trudy wanted to keep the baby. We were altar girls together. We prayed together every night. But, I convinced her to murder that baby."

"Honey," Rey said as she attempted to stop her. Sophie put her hand up in front of Rey's face.

"Wait!" Rey stopped to listen. "While my sister was on the table and they were murdering her baby, Trudy had a hemorrhagic stroke. She died on the way to the hospital."

Sophie did not cry but she appeared to be looking through Rey, almost comatose.

"So you're looking at a selfish, jealous, double murderer. Now you know why I don't go to communion. Because I don't deserve forgiveness."

Rey's eyes were starting to well up with tears.

"Don't cry," Sophie said. "It'll make me cry."

Rey dabbed her eyes with a tissue.

"You do deserve forgiveness. You've carried this burden around for too long."

"Do you think God would ever forgive me?"

"I know he would. Ask sincerely and with your heart," Rey shared.

"Will you help me?"

"What do you think? You're like a daughter to me, Sophia."

Sophie stood and clasped Rey in a tight hug.

For the first time since her sister's death, Sophie felt hope that she might be able to live life again. She did not want the hug to end nor did she want Rey to ever leave her.

CHAPTER 11

As darkness covered the landscape in El Cajon, Abdul finished a prayer session with the six men. He then handed them each a package that contained a Coghlan's Emergency Blanket. This was a polyester blanket that was approximately 7 feet by 5 feet and was aluminized to reflect body heat back to the body.

"I suggest wrapping yourself in it," Abdul advised. "Sleep now. In the morning, we will have our individual sessions."

The men all attempted to wrap the blankets around themselves while searching for a place on Abdul's living room floor to spend the night. The house was becoming chilly. Once a man found a location, the next task was trying to cover their head within the blanket to add warmth.

Abdul retreated to his bedroom and sat on the edge of the king-sized bed. It contained a plush down comforter and was fitted with 3,000 thread-count Egyptian sheets. Abdul reviewed the phone log on his cell phone and retrieved a stored number to call. It was answered on the second ring.

"Good evening, kind sir," said the voice. This was the voice that Jack heard during his car ride with Abdul.

"Are your people ready? Because mine are."

"They're ready."

"Then we meet tomorrow. I say 11:30. Come and pick me up and we'll take a ride. Be sure you bring everything you need," Abdul's voice was strident with authority.

"Can we do it later in the day?" the voice asked.

"No. I have to pick up my car in the afternoon in Carlsbad. I don't know when it will be ready."

"Do you want to do it after that?"

"This is not the time to be cheap. Park on the street. Call me when you get here."

Abdul rather curtly ended the call. He looked at his cell phone and then straight ahead with a sour, pensive stare. He followed it with a comment.

"You want something from me, Jew, then come and get it."

Day 2
WEDNESDAY

CHAPTER 12

The next morning, Rey was hopeful that her conversations with Jack and Sophie would change their perspective on forgiveness. They did not. All three went to church together, but Jack and Sophie did not partake in the communion offering. Jack dropped Rey off at the Dolphin Hotel and drove Sophie to the Laundromat Lounge with a bagful of bedding from Rey and Jack.

Jack proceeded to Thunderbar Buick. His luck in finding a parking spot this day was terrible. He had to park so far away from the dealership that another employee saw him and gave him a ride.

When he entered the dealership, he was immediately met by the Customer Service Manager, Bill Godfrey.

"This afternoon, you've got to go pick up that guy in El Cajon," Bill told him.

Jack did not respond, but appeared to be lost in thought.

"You want me to send Smitty?" Bill asked.

"No, no, it's all right. I'll go and get him. What time should I pick him up?" Jack wondered.

"We told him that his car would be ready by 4:00."

"Okay," Jack acknowledged. "No problem."

"Talk to Wally to see if he needs any parts to be picked up down that way."

Wally was the Parts Manager at the dealership. During the middle of the day, Jack would drop off and pick up parts from other dealerships in the County.

"Will do," Jack told him and proceeded to pick up the list of morning passengers.

As he scanned the list, his cell phone came to life. He glanced at the Caller ID and saw it was from Deke Cykes. He was Jack's friend, who previously worked for the CIA. Jack sent him a copy of the recording of his passenger's phone call and information regarding the passenger.

"Hey, what's going on?" Jack asked with interest and concern.

"We need to talk," Deke said in a less-than-ebullient voice.

"So, I guess it's not something that we can discuss over the phone?"

"No. It's better if we talk face-to-face. What's your schedule like?" Deke asked.

"I should be in the clear by 11:00 this morning."

"All right," Deke told him. "There's a Krispy Kreme donut place in the Clairemont Town Square shopping center on Clairemont Mesa Drive. I'll see you there at 11:30."

"Okay. I'll see you then."

Jack ended his call, but not the machinations of his mind. Whatever he had stumbled upon, his bigger concern was why he saw his passenger's face like an x-ray for a moment, the same way he saw it on his son four years earlier.

CHAPTER 13

Abdul spent the morning in a private session with each of the six men conscripted for the mission. The men were assured that their families would be cared for and they should have no concerns. Abdul spoke of paradise in detail as if he had been there before and that he was envious because he was not going with them.

When the last private session was completed, Abdul summoned the men together for a group session. They gathered around the dining room table, all dressed in white shirts, with no tie, black pants and polished black shoes.

"Gentlemen," Abdul began. "My father had a saying that was applicable to any undertaking. I want to share that with you now and discuss it."

Abdul's eyes moved slowly across the men as he spoke.

"If you want a plant to grow to full size, the weeds must be removed. Rafid do you know what that means?"

"The soil must be clean?"

"No," Abdul answered, rather irked.

"What do you think, Naseer?"

Naseer was the most quiet of the group, always intently listening.

"Any impediments to your project must be removed."

"Very good," Abdul responded. "You know, my father's saying sounds so much better in Farsi. Naseer, why don't you translate it for us."

"What?" Naseer questioned his request.

"I would like you to translate 'If you want a plant to grow to full size, the weeds must be removed', in Farsi."

Naseer thought for a moment, but Abdul again spoke up.

"No, wait. How about Hindu? Translate it for us in Hindu."

"I don't know what you are talking about," Naseer opined.

"My understanding is that you are a certified language translation specialist in Farsi, Hindu, and ten other languages. Gentlemen, meet FBI Special Agent Kenneth Williams."

As Abdul spoke the agent's name, the men to either side of him quickly stood and each pointed a SIG Sauer P220 .45 caliber semi-automatic pistol at his head. Abdul stopped for a moment to let the group take in the information. He then removed a pair of handcuffs from his back pocket and slid them across the table to Rafid.

"Hook him up," Abdul commanded. As Rafid placed the Special Agent in handcuffs, Abdul stared him down.

"You were recommended to us. The person who made the recommendation to us will be punished in kind. I select my martyrs based on raw nerve, not their ability to conjugate a verb."

Rafid put him in handcuffs and Abdul had an additional command.

"Take his shoes off. He's got a GPS tracking device in his right heel. One of you other men wear his shoes for now."

Rafid quickly complied.

"Mr. Williams, it appears that someone in your office is sympathetic to our cause. But you still only pursue people like us.

Now, I must share with you the price for your deception. Your mother, your father, your brothers, your sisters, your wife, your children, must all be put to death. All because of your foolish action. We are not going to kill you though. We need you to beg for it."

Abdul's cheeks bulged with a smile that filled his face.

"Gentlemen, I am going to teach you how we handled this situation in the old country. First, we are going to sever Mr. Williams' spinal cord in two places in the neck area. This takes precision. We are not severing the spine, but the nerve system encased in the vertebrae and discs. If done properly, he will have no ability to move any part of his body below the neck. We will then remove his tongue and his lower jaw."

"What about the GPS?" Rafid wondered.

"Men will be here in an hour to take him out to Arizona. They'll take the tracker with them." Abdul focused on the group. "Take him downstairs."

All the men scurried to oblige and Abdul considered his plan to be bulletproof. There was still much to do.

CHAPTER 14

Rory awoke on the floor of his apartment with no recollection as to how he had returned home. His memory of the evening before was that he purchased two 'hits' of methamphetamine from a dealer near the Oceanside Pier. He found an alcove on the side of a building off Mission Avenue and began the process of ingesting both of them. After that, his mind was wiped clean.

The door to his apartment was wide open and anyone walking by would most likely think that he walked in and collapsed. Rory slowly moved to an 'all fours' position when he realized that his captive, Carol Ann Zelinsky, was in the closet.

He moved like the apartment was on fire, racing to the closet door and sliding the three deadbolts. After opening the door and pushing back the clothes, there swung Carol Ann from the closet rod, weakened from a lack of food and water, using most of her energy to raise her head.

Rory did not utter a word. He first sauntered over to his apartment door and slammed it closed, cringing at the noise. Then he grabbed his backpack and began to search through it. From it, he retrieved a large, unopened Snickers bar. Walking back to the closet, Rory produced from his pocket a four-inch folding knife and flipped it open.

He reached the entrance to the closet and stared at her for a moment.

"Hold still," he told her as he pulled on the duct tape and cut a line down it. He then peeled it back from her mouth.

Rory tore open the packaging at one end of the Snickers bar and put the chocolate close to her mouth, so she could take a bite. He put the rest of the bar in her hand.

"I'll leave the door open for a little while, so you can see what you're doing."

"Listen," Carol said in an extremely weakened voice, "I was thinking maybe you're right. Maybe we could be together."

Rory smiled at her, nodded his head, and walked to the kitchen. He snatched the fish food from the counter and began to sprinkle flakes into the fish tank. As he was performing this task, he spotted his cell phone.

He seized the phone from the floor and looked up a number from his contact list. He pushed a button to call the number. It was answered on the fourth ring.

"Hey, Zee, it's me, Rory." A moment passed. "Nothin', I'm still on disability. Listen, I need to borrow your truck." Another moment passed. "I'll put gas in it." Rory continued to listen. "Yeah. What time?" He waited for an answer. "All right. I'll see ya then. Hey Zee, I also need a shovel."

Carol Ann heard every word of the conversation as she wolfed down the last bite of her Snickers bar. When she heard the word 'shovel,' alarm bells blasted in her mind. It was now time for fight or flight.

CHAPTER 15

At approximately 11:25 am, Jack pulled into the parking lot of the Krispy Kreme located on Clairemont Mesa Drive. He scurried inside and gave the place a quick visual scan in search of Deke Cykes. The interior was a beaming white with red, trim tile to accent it. His scan bore fruit.

At the farthest table from the ordering area sat Deke munching on the final bite of a glazed donut. He was 62 years old, a full head of gray hair, 215 pounds, and had a very intimidating look when he wasn't smiling. Deke saw Jack and he waved him over.

Deke stood as Jack approached and they met with a quick, tight hug.

"My brother," Jack told him.

"You don't look too bad for a bus driver," Deke told him with a smile.

"I'm a shuttle driver," Jack conveyed as both men sat across from each other. Deke had already purchased coffee for both of them.

"You still take your coffee black?" Deke wondered.

"Yep."

"Well, I got us both a donut, but your donut started calling my name and, you know, donuts are like my kryptonite."

"You gotta do what you gotta do," Jack told him.

"I passed that conversation along to one of my associates at the Company. It does have some interesting stuff on it."

"Like what?" Jack wondered.

"First of all, the guy in your vehicle was talking Farsi. The guy he was talking to was speaking Hebrew."

"I wouldn't think that would be very common," Jack conveyed.

"Neither would I," Deke told him. "The substance of the conversation involved the grooming of dogs and the purchasing of collars and harnesses for dogs."

"Do you think it's code for something?" Jack speculated.

"Maybe," Deke concurred. "But your boy, Abdul Muhsi, is a retired history professor and his daughter and son-in-law run a dog grooming business that caters to show dogs for high-end customers."

"No criminal background on that guy?"

"They got one hit. He was suspected of funneling cash to a sleeper cell in Orlando, Florida. It was purely anecdotal. Nobody talked and they had no proof."

"What about the other guy?"

"They ran a voice recognition test on him. Nothing."

"But why would that guy, Abdul, warn the other guy about a backdoor trace, no record of the call, and that it can't be intercepted?"

"Listen, in this day and age, everybody is worrying about the government being a peeping Tom. They get paranoid. Especially, these people. They're always being racially profiled. You're racially profiling them now."

"All I'm telling you is: these guys are up to something. I know it, Deke."

"Jack, the government appreciates your vigilance. But let me tell you what they told me to tell you. Let it go. The CIA has files on a lot more people than just those in the Middle East. They knew about your alcohol problem and they knew about your drug problem. I told them you were clean, but it muddies the water."

Jack looked at him in frustration.

"Is there anything coming up in the San Diego area that would be considered a target for a terrorist attack?"

"I asked the same question," Deke told him. "One is a convention that begins tomorrow of the International Conference of Chabad-Lubavitch Emissaries. The FBI has eyes on it and security will be as tight as if the President was there. That would be the place if a terrorist cell wanted make a stand. The other is a speech being given by the top negotiator for the proposed Palestinian-Israeli peace talks, whenever they get off the ground. That takes place at the Jewish Academy near the 56 and Carmel Creek Road."

Deke was referring to Interstate 56 in the Carmel Del Mar area of San Diego.

"They gonna have security there?"

"Not as tight as the first place, but they will have boots on the ground."

Jack nodded his head in thought.

"Are you satisfied?" Deke asked.

"Well," Jack replied reluctantly, "I guess."

"Jack, listen to me. Anybody who knows you as well as I do, knows that you have a death wish. Don't get any ideas and try to go lone wolf on this thing. Because if there is something there, these are dangerous people. Don't get in the middle of it."

"No, I hear you." Jack conceded.

"We good then?"

"We're great."

"All right, then. My wife and I are taking a trip up the coast to Santa Barbara. I told her that I would turn off my cell and leave it home. You know what else I told her?"

"That you were going to bring her home donuts. Come on, my treat."

Jack and Deke rose from the table and proceeded to the ordering area. Jack was trying to convince himself that Abdul was a simple dog groomer, but he was failing miserably at it.

CHAPTER 16

Eighteen miles away from the Krispy Kreme donut shop, Abdul strolled down Mollison Avenue looking for his ride. As promised, it appeared at exactly 11:30 am.

The late model, red Bentley was factory clean as if it had just been driven off the showroom floor. The interior was a crème color and burl wood accented the dashboard and doors.

Abdul opened the door and slid in quickly. As soon as Abdul closed the door, the car was in motion. The driver was Ibrahim Bergsteen, an Israeli National who came to America thirty years earlier to learn the Jewelry trade. Ibrahim went by the name 'Izzie' and operated a high-end jewelry store in La Jolla on Prospect Avenue, the main drag of the town.

Izzie was 68 years old, bald with a fringe of white hair. He was short and weighed nearly 300 pounds.

Both men looked straight ahead as they spoke.

"How's my favorite jeweler?" Abdul asked.

"Good," Izzie answered. "Soon to be better."

"So, your people are ready?"

"That's what they tell me."

"For the kind of money that you're paying, you better be definite," replied Abdul.

"Don't worry, my friend. You're just the diversion. We want a lot of cops in the opposite direction."

"Does it bother you that thousands of your people will end up dead tomorrow?" Abdul quizzed.

"You know, Al, I've done a lot of things in my life, but the one thing I do best is survive. Whatever it takes to maintain my survival is the price that others have to pay."

"You got what you came to bring me?"

"It's in the trunk. Three-fifty large. In cash," Izzie advised.

Izzie was telling Abdul that there was $350,000 in cash in a suitcase in the trunk of his car.

"Get the other half ready," Abdul told him.

"You going to give it a little time to cool down?"

"No. Get it ready. And don't make me come looking for you. Take me back."

Abdul was done speaking. They had merely circled two city blocks before returning to Abdul's townhouse. Izzie popped the trunk and Abdul removed the suitcase. Half of Abdul's payment had now been made for the larger plan.

CHAPTER 17

Back in Oceanside, the temperature had reached 78 degrees, but a cool breeze off the ocean gave the air a comfortable, warm flow. At the Laundromat Lounge, Sophie had just finished her washing, drying, and folding of Rey and Jack's bedding. All that was left was packaging it for transport.

There were three customers taking care of their once dirty clothes: one was waiting on a washer and the other two were waiting on dryers. It was then that Rory entered. He stopped for a moment to shove his shoelaces into his sneakers, which he never tied.

He carried a duffel bag of dirty clothes and scanned the establishment before deciding which machine to use. He looked for Sophie, but she was not in sight. Rory selected a washing machine close to the office where Sophie scurried to when they had their last encounter.

He loaded the machine and checked the change in his pocket. The cost to operate the machine was $2.25. Rory proceeded to the dollar changer and made change for two, one dollar bills. Before he deposited any money in the machine, he went to the back office in search of Sophie. He found her in a work area that was used for the

Fluff & Fold folding. It had no windows and only one door for entry and exit.

"Excuse me," Rory spoke up to gain her attention.

She looked up, slightly startled, and stared at him.

"Can you help me? I don't know if I'm using the right washer for the clothes I'm trying to wash."

Sophie had string in hand that she was using to bind the wrapping on the clean sheets. Also within reach was a large scissors, used to cut the string. Sophie resisted the urge to grab the scissors.

"Show me what machine you're using."

She followed him out into the laundry area and he showed her the machine. She looked into it.

"That one's fine. Don't use too much soap."

"Okay," Rory said sheepishly. "I'm sorry about the other day if I made you nervous."

"It's all right," Sophie told him and proceeded to slowly back away from him. Before taking up residence in the office, she retrieved the scissors.

For the next two hours, Rory sat in focused solitude as the machines washed and dried his clothes. When they were done being dried, he did not fold them – but simply crammed them into his duffel bag.

Sophie spent the time watching him and praying. She wondered why he was not leaving. It was then that she decided to take action. She went to the telephone and punched a speed dial button.

"Nine-one-one, what is your emergency?"

"I don't know if this is an emergency, but I work at the Laundromat Lounge on South Coast Highway. There is a man here who washed his clothes and is not leaving. He was here the other night and asked me to go on a date."

"We have a unit in route. The estimated time of arrival is one minute."

As promised, an Oceanside police cruiser pulled up in front of the Laundromat. A police officer moved quickly to the front door and entered. A quick visual check by the officer established that Rory was the only one not involved with washing or drying clothes.

As soon as Rory saw the officer, he stood to leave.

"Come here," the officer called out to him. "Let me see your I.D."

Sophie came out of the office as soon as she saw the police officer. Rory complied with the officer's commands acting as if nothing was wrong. As he was escorted out, he shot a glance at Sophie that put a knot of fear in her gut.

CHAPTER 18

At Abdul's townhome, three men arrived to remove the traitor that Abdul had discovered. Special Agent Kenneth Williams had been surgically sliced at the hands of Abdul and his wounds covered with duct tape. His prognosis for survival was dim.

Any item of clothing that was bloodstained was removed and taken away by the men. Their destination was the Arizona desert. Abdul directed them to leave the special agent in one location and take his shoe, with the GPS tracker approximately 50 miles away, and put it in a dumpster.

Once the men left, Abdul decided that it was time for another session of the history of the world according to Abdul.

All the men were once again nicely dressed in the white shirts and dark slacks. Abdul directed them to sit at his dining room table while he stood at the head of it to deliver his lecture.

"History," he began, "should never be ignored. When studied, you truly see a pattern, an identifiable cycle that either will provide hope or dismal fear that actions, which took place long ago, will return."

Abdul surveyed the men.

"Our actions are taken for the glory of Allah. But if you look back in history, men such as Adolf Hitler and his Final Solution attempted to achieve the same goal: extermination and eradication of a plague that is the bane of our very existence. An infection that must be annihilated for our survival and the benefit of the entire world.

"The powers of the world underestimate us, and it is from this that our power emanates. The United States engages in self-deception. They think we can be stopped and they know everything. But they don't. We are like the cockroach that scurries when the light goes on. While you might kill a few, most get away. And if you were to set off a nuclear bomb, we, like the cockroach, are the only ones to survive."

Abdul stopped for a moment to allow the men to absorb his message.

"Back to Hitler for a moment, while his attempt was noble, his execution was flawed. Does anyone know why Hitler's Final Solution was unsuccessful?"

The room was quiet.

"Because his reach exceeded his grasp. Hitler wanted to rule the world. His priorities were not properly defined. If he had approached it on a country-by-country basis; cleansing a particular country before moving on to the next one, then his success would have been achieved. By trying to cleanse all of Europe at once, his efforts were doomed to failure."

Rafid decided to interject a question.

"I hear them called Christ-killers. Did they kill the one called Christ?"

"In all honesty," Abdul declared, "they did not. They had the Romans do it for them. This is the nature of the beast. They flex their financial muscle to buy partners and protectors like the United

States to hide behind. This is why we must take action like that which we will undertake tomorrow. It is necessary for our survival and the glory of Allah."

Abdul was done speaking. He knew that his men were primed and captivated. They were ready to go now. The men believed that, in less than 24 hours, history would be written in blood.

CHAPTER 19

Near the corner of Miramar Road and Camino Santa Fe in the northern portion of the San Diego city limits, sat Bud's British Import. It was a small car repair facility that catered to owners of Jaguars, Triumphs, Land Rovers, and the occasional Bentley or Rolls Royce.

The facility consisted of a small warehouse, with six overhead doors on the front, and a small, glass-walled showroom on the southern end.

When a late model, red Bentley pulled in, it caused no additional attention until its driver stepped out of the vehicle. It was Izzie Bergsteen, the jeweler who met with Abdul earlier in the day to make a fifty percent down payment on a covert criminal enterprise.

Izzie stood near the car and waited for someone to approach him. A young man, in his early 20s appeared and before he reached Izzie, Izzie called out to him.

"Tell Ace I'm here."

The young man turned around and made haste back through the showroom door. Within two minutes, one of the overhead doors opened and the same young man called out to Izzie.

"Pull it in."

Izzie obliged and the overhead door was closed as soon as the car cleared the threshold of the door. Izzie again exited the vehicle and continued to keep the car within sight.

A tall, thin, dark-skinned man of African descent, but born in London, approached him with a broad smile as he wiped his newly washed hands. He wore blue coveralls and the name over his left breast that read 'Ace.'

"Jolly good to see you, mate," Ace told Izzie with a defined British accent.

"How you doing, Ace?"

"The bee's knees. I was right about to ring you up. Come to bring me a present, did ya?"

Ace was indicating the he was having a great day and he was about to call Izzie on the phone.

"In the trunk," Izzie responded.

They both walked around to the back of the car and Izzie popped the trunk open using his key fob. When they reached the back of the car, Ace saw the large, silver-metal suitcase.

"Check it," Izzie told him.

Ace clicked open the two latches of the suitcase and opened it. It was filled with neatly placed, banded $100 bills. Ace pivoted his head to Izzie.

"Crikey. I don't have to count it, do I, mate?"

Izzie shook his head with a negative stride.

"Five hundred, twenty-five thousand. Seventy-five percent of seven hundred thousand."

Ace stood and closed the lid of the suitcase. He spoke as he clicked the latches.

"Me and my mates are ready to go."

"Tomorrow. Three thirty. Don't contact me. I'll look for it on the news."

Ace hauled the bag out of the trunk and set it down on the four wheels attached to the bag. He rolled it slightly away from the car while Izzie was able to close the trunk using his key. Then, Ace extended his hand to Izzie.

"Pleasure doing business with you, Izzie," Ace said as they shook hands.

"Likewise," Izzie responded.

"You remember why I asked for seventy-five percent on this job instead of fifty?"

"Yeah."

"I'd hate to have to come lookin' for ya, mate."

"I'm not going anywhere."

Ace shook his head in acknowledgment and turned to the original young man and gave him the signal to raise the overhead door. Izzie backed out and Ace waved goodbye. Ace then waited for the overhead door to come back down.

"You got it?" Ace called out to a corner of the garage.

"Every word," a voice responded.

All the money that was to be paid prior to the event had now changed hands.

CHAPTER 20

3 WEEKS EARLIER

Izzie and his red Bentley made an unexpected visit to Bud's British Import. He parked in the customer parking area and strolled inside. He was greeted by a young lady wearing a mini-skirt and rather snug shirt that advertised her assets.

"May I be of assistance, sir?" she asked with a forced British accent.

"Is Ace here?"

"I believe he's in the *ga-roge* (garage). I'll call him," she offered.

"No need," Izzie told her decisively and sauntered over to the door for entrance to the garage.

"Sir, customers aren't allowed in there."

Izzie ignored her. He strolled through the twelve bays of the garage and gave a cursory glance to several of the mechanics working on cars. He stopped when he saw the legs of Ace under a Triumph Spider TR7. He approached the legs and gave Ace's foot a slight tap. Ace wheeled his mechanic creeper out from under the car and was slightly surprised to see his guest.

"As I live and breathe. Is this a social call? Were you just in the neighborhood?"

"You got someplace where we can talk?" Izzie asked.

"In the back," Ace told him before calling over to one of the other mechanics. "Baz, can you finish up on this Triumph?"

Ace grabbed a cloth to wipe his hands and Izzie followed into a small office in the back of the building. It was sterile, rather non-descript, with furniture that was at least forty years old. Ace closed the door after Izzie entered.

"Have a seat," Ace offered. "Can I get you something to drink?"

"I'm good."

"What can I do you for today, Izzie, old chap?"

Ace posed his inquiry as he sat at the desk.

"I got a job I think you might be interested in," Izzie shared.

"You know me. I'm always interested in decent, hard work. What's the job, my jeweler friend?"

"I want you to rob a bank over in La Jolla. Sunset Savings on Torrey Pines Road."

"You want me and my mates to rob a bank for you?" Ace spoke in disbelief. "I think you're losing your marbles."

"I'm willing to pay $700,000 for the job. All I want is for you to go in there and get one item out of a safe deposit box."

Ace was intrigued by the dollar amount.

"What is this item?"

"A Chase & Sanborn coffee can."

"What is in this coffee can? I suspect it is something other than coffee?"

"Diamonds. A former partner and I had an agreement to purchase them from a South African investor. My partner backed out on me, then I found out that he proceeded to consummate the deal without me."

"What are they? Large stones or something else?"

"Something else. It's got a red diamond, pink diamond, blue diamond, and yellow diamond. Not the largest in the world, but very close. I'm told the can is filled with some extraordinary sizes and cuts."

"You're an interesting jeweler, mate," Ace responded.

"A jeweler will tell you that when valuing a diamond, you must look at the '4 Cs': color, cut, clarity, and carat weight. I tell you there is a fifth 'C' and it is the most important one: cash. That's what these diamonds will bring."

Ace contemplated Izzie's comments.

"Bank robberies are tough these days," Ace imparted. "A lot of cameras, armed security, and cops never too far away."

"All you have to do is get this can out of the safe deposit box. I'll have an inside person there, she works for the bank. Just get the can into her purse. Then, you and your buddies get out of Dodge."

"Why don't you just have your inside person pinch it?"

"No. They would know it was an inside job."

"I don't see a problem with snagging it. The problem is an escape plan," Ace ruminated.

"I'm going to help you with that," Izzie declared. "I've got this Middle Eastern guy, who is planning a bombing at a Jewish event in three weeks. You coordinate the robbery at the same time with the bombing and you will have every cop in the city heading in the opposite direction, away from the bank."

"You sure this Middle Eastern guy is going to go through with this bombing?"

"I'm financing it," Izzie proudly proclaimed. "But it's dependent on you saying 'yes.'"

Ace once again thought for a moment.

"I'm a little concerned about walking out of there empty handed," Ace advised.

"I'll give you half the money the day before. But it's got to be in cash."

Ace stared at Izzie while the wheels in his mind spun.

"I'll tell you what," Ace countered, "make it seventy-five percent up front, you got a deal."

"What, you don't trust me?" Izzie said in shocked disbelief and exaggerated hand gestures. "Haven't I always treated you good? Who do you come to when you need a local fence?"

Izzie had developed a criminal clientele thanks to his wholesale sideline for the fencing of recently stolen jewels. Ace was one of the few criminal clients that Izzie trusted.

"It's got nothing to do with trust, Iz. I gotta take care a me mates."

"Look, when you bring me something and it's paste, I tell you it's paste. But if it's ice, and it's good ice, I pay you top dollar."

Izzie was pointing out to Ace that some jewelry was costume jewelry and therefore, of little value. But if it was a good diamond or 'ice', Izzie paid the fair market value.

"You know your onions about ice. My concern," Ace shared, "is that once you get the item you're seeking, this coffee can, you won't be in a hurry to pay the balance. That one time you went to Tel Aviv, or some godforsaken place, for two months before we got paid."

"That was a miscommunication," Izzie declared.

"Seventy-five percent and the balance within 48 hours after the job. We got a deal?"

Izzie stood and extended his hand to Ace. Ace shook his hand and then handed him a folded piece of paper.

"Deal. Let's keep our communications to a minimum. I'll contact you. Three weeks from tomorrow – Thursday. At 3:30. I'll get you the payment three weeks from today. This," Izzie said, referring to the piece of paper, "is the number of the box, the inside lady's first name, and the date and time for the event. That should be sufficient.

Ace scanned the piece of paper.

"A fortnight and a week. I'll give you a little slack on the first payment. But Izzie, don't make me come looking for it. That would place a serious strain on our relationship."

"Don't worry. With what this Middle Eastern guy's got planned, your heist will look like a convenience store robbery."

"Let's hope so. I'll walk you out."

Both men exited the office and did not speak again until they reached Izzie's car.

"Take care, Izzie."

"You too, Ace."

Izzie now planned to invest $700,000 with Abdul for a terrorist event and $700,000 with Ace for the bank robbery. The wheels for the culmination of all events were now in motion.

CHAPTER 21

Later that evening, Ace assembled his team. He selected four men who worked at Bud's British Import and each provided a unique skill. They met in a sales conference room after closing hours.

"Gentlemen," Ace began, "I've been presented with a job. A bank job on the outskirts of La Jolla, near the freeway. Basic take down. We're only going in to get one item. We don't walk out with it. We slip it to the inside person and we're done."

"What's the one item: a vault?" one of the men, Baz, exclaimed with a laugh.

Baz was 6 feet, 1 inch tall with a solid frame. His expertise was in welding, especially in delicate situations.

"It's a coffee can inside a safe deposit box. What do we need to get in it, Baz?"

"Send Tina tomorrow to open up an account and sign up for a safe deposit box," Baz relayed. "Tell her to get photos of the room and tighter shots on the boxes. I need to see the hinges and the interior of the locking mechanism."

"Done," Ace concurred. "We'll also get photos of the lobby and I'll do a sketch of the layout. Baz, how long do you think to get in the box?"

"I can cut the face of it off in two minutes or less."

"All right. Time is gonna be precious."

"You said there was an inside man," chimed Rick, whose birth name was Cedric, and claimed an expertise in opening safes and vaults. "If you can get the bank key, the renter's key is a five pinner with one security pin. I can pick it within 30 seconds."

"Let me see what I can do about that," Ace shared. "Reggie, we're going to need three fast cars."

"Fast enough to beat the rozzers, I suspect?" Reggie wondered.

The 'rozzers' were British slang for policemen.

"You got it, mate," Ace told him. "This is what I'm thinking on that angle. Once we get out a there, we each go in a different direction: north, south, and east. There's a commercial safe house within five miles of this place within each direction. They all have underground parking. Even if they have the whirly birds after us, once we're in the buildings, we should be clean."

The whirly birds that Ace referred to were helicopters.

"What's a 'commercial' safe house?" Reggie quizzed.

"These are buildings that were built with an underground vault that is not seen on any architectural plans. The cops can search the building all day long and they'll never find it. A person can live in it for up to a year."

"Who owns these buildings?" Reggie wondered.

"Someone with an extreme dislike of the government," Ace disclosed. "Once we make it to the vaults, we communicate through Rudy in El Paso. He'll extract us from the buildings on an individual basis."

"What's the take down for this exercise?" Baz inquired.

"Seven hundred thousand," Ace relayed.

"Who's the numpty paying the freight for this thing?" Rick demanded.

A numpty was British slang for an incompetent or unwise person.

"Izzie the Fence."

"He's all mouth and no trousers, that guy is." Rick proclaimed.

"From this point forward," Ace added, "whenever I talk to this guy, I want sound and video. If any of us get pinched, we cut a deal selling out Mr. Fence."

All the men nodded in agreement.

"Well, knees up, boys. We're gonna be rocking and rolling," Ace assured them.

The men continued to discuss minor details, but they had confidence in their plan and in their leader. At Sunrise Savings, they were unaware that 'the British are coming.'

CHAPTER 22

As the sun blazed down on the El Cajon landscape, Jack pulled up in front of Abdul's townhome on North Mollison Avenue just a few minutes after 3:00 pm. Abdul stood in the shade of a nearby tree, with sand-colored slacks and a blue, short-sleeve, open neck button shirt. As soon as Jack stopped along the curbside, Abdul wasted no time getting into the back seat of the vehicle.

"How are you, my friend?" Abdul inquired in a rather ebullient voice.

Jack put the vehicle in park, took off his sunglasses, and turned around to shake hands with his guest. Once again, in the blink of an eye, Abdul's face appeared as an x-ray.

"I'm fine. How are you?" Jack asked, now able to minimize his amazement at what he just witnessed.

"Very good, my friend."

"Let's go get your car."

The SUV courtesy shuttle began the journey back to Thunderbar Buick. For the first few minutes, the ride was quiet. Abdul looked out the window, while Jack focused on driving.

"Would you like me to put on the radio?" Jack wondered.

"I'm fine, my friend. If you would like it on, feel free."

"I prefer the peace and quiet."

"A man after my own heart."

A few moments passed. The vehicle made its way to the North Mollison Avenue exit on Interstate 8 and headed west. Abdul decided to interrupt the silence.

"My friend, can I ask you a favor?"

"Sure," Jack responded.

"Can we take the fifteen to the fifty-six? Then across the fifty-six to the five?"

Abdul was asking Jack to drive north on Interstate 15, west on Interstate 56, then north on Interstate 5 to Carlsbad. This was one of several ways to arrive at the dealership in Carlsbad.

"No problem," Jack told him. "Are you wondering about the traffic?"

"Yes. I have to cut across the fifty-six tomorrow around this time."

"Oh, yeah. What exit?"

"Carmel Creek Road," Abdul nonchalantly disclosed.

Jack suddenly became lost in focus. Abdul was speaking but Jack was not registering a word of it. If there were sirens attached to Jack's head, they would be blaring at this moment.

One of the locations provided by Jack's friend, Deke, for a possible terrorist event, was the San Diego Jewish Academy located near the Carmel Creek Road exit. Jack now knew the location of the event planned by Abdul.

Jack's stratagem as to what action to take remained murky. Deke was not available for counsel because he was taking his wife to Santa Barbara and could not be reached by phone. Jack wondered who he could call to assist in uncovering a plot for which he really did not have much information.

CHAPTER 23

While Rory was cleaning his laundry and having a discussion with the Oceanside Police, his prisoner, Carol Ann Zelinsky, continued her escape efforts. For hours, she smashed one of her feet into the same soundproof panel in an effort to break through it. She could feel slight movement every time she hit it. Then with one angry, explosive hit, she heard the panel crack.

The soundproofing material acted as a camouflage to cover the broken plasterboard. Carol Ann stopped to regain her breath when she heard the deadbolts begin to slide.

The closet door opened and the clothes were slid over. Rory looked at her as if he was studying an oddity. He looked her up and down, pivoting his head to the left then right. Then Rory decided to speak.

"I don't like your hair. It looks like a boy."

Carol Ann's pageboy haircut was taped down by the duct tape. She made several noises in an attempt to communicate with Rory.

"I'm gonna go get you another candy bar," he said with deadpan inflection. "I'm gonna let you go tomorrow. Or I might give you to a friend of mine. I haven't decided."

Carol Ann had no faith in Rory's promise. She was running out of time to make her escape.

CHAPTER 24

When Jack and Abdul returned to the Buick dealership, each went their separate way. Abdul paid his bill and commenced his long trek back to El Cajon. Jack had a list of part requests for pick up the next day. He would place them in a logical sequence so that he and the other shuttle courtesy driver, Smitty, had a route to follow after all the shuttle customers were returned home.

There were nine requests for parts at five different locations and he assigned the entire list to Smitty. Jack would only be responsible for customer transport the next day.

While sitting at his cubicle, Jack began his research. He began with an internet search for 'Homeland Security.' He found a section labeled 'Report Incidents.' Then, he found two interesting sections, one labeled 'Report Criminal Activity' and the other 'Report Terror Activity.'

Jack had a slight hesitation because he did not have sufficient information to know exactly what was going on. The section dealing with Terror Activity advised people to contact their local FBI office.

He found the telephone number for the local office located on Vista Sorrento Parkway in San Diego. He lifted the receiver on his desk phone, but before he pushed a number on the keypad, he felt inhibited about what he was doing. What if Abdul was a simple dog groomer or provider of dog supplies? Perhaps, Jack thought, he was racially profiling him.

Jack returned the receiver to its cradle and was torn about what he should do next. His friend, Deke, relayed to him that the government knew about his past drinking and drug abuse problems. He feared that with the information he possessed regarding Abdul, they would consider him a crackpot drunk or a doped-out pill-popper. Jack decided to sleep on it and make a decision in the morning.

What Jack really feared was that the government would not take him seriously. If that was the case, what could he do to stop Abdul?

CHAPTER 25

At 6:45 pm, Sophie began preparations to close down the Laundromat Lounge for the day. She would check each washer and dryer and remove any unattended clothes. People would often start a load of clothes, then run errands, and return after the laundromat was closed.

She went through all of the machines and locked the front door. Jack had promised to pick her up this day to help carry home the bedding for Rey and Jack that she had washed and dried. Sophie entered the rear office and made sure all the video monitors were on. As she swiftly turned to exit, there stood Rory.

At first, Sophie was alarmed and stunned by his presence. Before she said a word, he spoke.

"I come in peace."

Sophie raised her palms toward him, giving the body language indication that she wanted to push him back.

"We're closed. You should leave. Now."

"I just wanted to apologize for earlier today. I don't want any trouble."

"Listen. Leave now or I'm going to call the police," Sophie was not timid, but rather adamant.

"No," Rory told her in a quiet, monotone voice. "That's a bad idea. You and I are going to talk."

As Rory finished his sentence, a loud banging was heard at the front door. Rory turned to look and Sophie darted past him out to the machine area of the laundromat. Jack was at the front door.

She raced to the door, led by her key, and unlocked it in record time. Jack could see that she was distressed.

"Jack, there's somebody in here. The same guy I told you about yesterday. I had to call the cops earlier today to get him out."

"Where is he?" Jack commanded like a big game hunter preparing for a kill shot.

Sophie pointed to the back office. Jack handed her his cell phone.

"If this guy tries anything, I want you to go outside, lock us in here, and call nine-one-one. Okay?"

She shook her head in acknowledgement. Jack turned and there stood Rory. No more than twenty feet away from him. The moment that Jack laid eyes on Rory, his face appeared as an x-ray.

"Who's this, Sophie, your grandfather?" Rory asked derisively.

"Why don't we step outside and I'll show you," Jack promised.

"Shouldn't you be playing bingo somewhere?" Rory replied in an attempt to be witty.

"Sophie, where do you think he falls on the autism scale? Because I don't think he's very high functioning."

The comment brought a smile to Sophie's face. When Rory caught a glimpse of it, from his pocket, he pulled out his knife with its four-inch blade and snapped it open.

"If you think," Jack began, "that you are going to scare me or intimidate me, you're wrong. If you want to go at it, right here, right now, let's do it. Because I don't want to stop you. I won't stop until one of us is dead. So, are you ready to die?"

Rory stared at Jack, not knowing how to respond to his words. Sophie broke the deadlock.

"Just get out of here!" demanded Sophie.

Rory walked down a different row of machines and out the front door. Both Jack and Sophie watched him walk away.

"Next time you see him," Jack advised, "before you do anything, call nine-one-one and get him trespassed off the property. This way the police can arrest him whenever he shows up."

"Okay," Sophie replied. "Let me get the bedding."

She went to the back and picked up the two packages. Sophie brought them to the front and Jack took them from her. She switched off the lights and locked the front door.

Jack and Sophie rode in silence in Jack's Honda Accord to the Dolphin Hotel. Sophie had just caught a glimpse of Jack's potential rage and she feared what he would do, if pushed to the limit.

CHAPTER 26

At the Dolphin Hotel, the bell on Rey's microwave indicated that her dinner was ready. Within a few moments, there was a knock at her door.

"Come on in," she called out and Jack and Sophie entered.

"We come bearing gifts," Jack told her and he set the packages of clean bedding on the counter near the microwave.

"I made stew and I hope you guys are hungry," Rey told them and they both smiled brightly.

"How do you do it, Rey? We don't have stoves or ovens?" Jack wondered.

"I have a friend, Dora, she only lives about two blocks away and she lets me use her stove. So, all I have to do is heat it up."

"You're incredible," Sophie said.

"I also have some crescent rolls that are still a little warm."

"How about tomorrow night, I take us all out to dinner, my treat?" Jack offered.

"No," Rey said, "that's too much."

"My treat, no discussion."

Rey eyed Jack with a smirk. Jack then opened a card table and Sophie breezed over to her apartment to grab a chair. When she returned, the table was quickly set. Rey put out the food and they sat.

"Who is going to say grace?"

"It's your house, my dear," Jack conveyed. "So, I think either you should say it or you should select the person to say it."

"That sounds like a good idea," Rey concurred. "How about Sophie?"

All three made the Sign of the Cross and Sophie began the prayer.

"Bless us, O Lord, for these thy gifts that we are about to receive from thy bounty through Christ, our Lord, amen."

Rey beamed a broad smile.

"How were your days, you two?"

"That same guy that I had a problem with yesterday, came in again today," Sophie told her. "I was really getting nervous, because I locked the door, then I see the guy is still inside. I was getting a very bad vibe from the guy. I don't know what would have happened if Jack hadn't shown up?"

"Well, I am going to come and pick you up at night," Jack told her.

"That's not necessary," Sophie told him.

"When I saw that guy, I saw something evil in him. I don't want you to take any chances."

"Thanks," Sophie said with relief.

"What about you, Jack?" Rey inquired. "How was your day?"

"Pensive."

"Share," Rey requested.

"I picked up my passenger from El Cajon today and he was interested in a particular location and time for tomorrow. I found it very troubling."

"What did you do about it?" Rey again inquired.

"Nothing. I was thinking that maybe, it was just a big misunderstanding on my part."

"There is a famous saying," Rey shared, "All that is necessary for the triumph of evil is that good men do nothing."

Jack looked down at his plate and had no response. He sighed. Sophie touched his forearm.

"Let it go. Don't let it torture you. There is enough torture in life without you looking for more."

"Is that why you go to church every day, Sophie?" Rey quizzed. "To escape torture."

"I love going to church. It's peaceful. Harmonious. For me, it's a place of sanctuary. It's a place of safety from the evil of the world."

"What about you, Jack?" Rey posed her inquiry. "Why do you go to church?"

Jack was slow to respond.

"In life, you must have a spiritual side. If you don't, your life is missing something. Most people don't even realize it. They wonder why life is empty. But they have the power to fill it."

Jack then started to chuckle.

"I'm thinking back to my lawyer days."

"You were a lawyer?" Sophie responded with surprised awe.

"It's hard for me to believe, too. But I didn't answer your question, Rey. About why I go to church every day. First of all, I go to pray for my family. Then, I'm always amazed at how much I learn from scripture and Gospel readings. No matter how many times I've heard it, it is still fresh to me. That is the power of the Bible's words."

"Amen," Rey answered.

"That's beautiful, Jack," Sophie concurred.

"Why do you go to church, Rey?" Jack wondered.

"I want to tell you both something. Jesus came to save us and he gave his life to do it. When you go to church, you are reminded of the grace that God offers to us in this life. While on earth, you should accept the graces from God. The grace to be forgiven, the grace to love, and the grace of the Eucharist, to be a part of Jesus himself. Everything is a grace."

Rey became more stern as she spoke.

"By refusing to take communion, you are judging yourselves and you have no right to do so. On Judgment Day, there will be two witnesses to judge you: your conscience and the Word of God. And it is your conscience with which you must make peace. Because by that time, your actions, upon which you will be judged, will be written in stone."

Rey's words echoed with Jack and Sophie. It was a simple, convincing argument. It was a cause for reflection. Sophie thought that Rey should have been a nun. Jack wondered if she was speaking directly about his situation involving Abdul.

Day 3
THURSDAY

CHAPTER 27

The church bells of St. Mary, Star of the Sea chimed out eight times. The daily mass had begun with Rey, Jack, and Sophie in attendance. They sat in their usual pew, which was the second one from the rear of the church. The center aisle to the altar area seemed farther away today for some reason, most likely because of the plethora of attendees from a variety of different social and financial strata.

Father Gerardo Fernandez celebrated the Mass as Rey, Jack, and Sophie listened intently. When the time came to approach the altar and receive the communion bread and wine, once again only Rey elected to join all the other parishioners. She anticipated that today would be the day that Jack and Sophie would follow her. But that did not appear to be the case.

When Rey received the sacrament, she looked to the large crucifix situated behind the altar and she asked Jesus to help them see and help them hear. She then moved to the right, walking up the side aisle for a return path to her seat.

After the last person received the sacrament, Father Fernandez turned to walk behind the altar and, after his second step, a voice reverberated from the back of the church.

"Excuse me!"

It was Jack following closely behind Sophie moving at a quick marching pace in double time. Today was the day that they would both take the sacrament after so many years.

Rey waited for them at the end of the pew before stepping in. All three kneeled, with Sophie to Rey's left and Jack on the right. Rey gave Sophie a quick kiss on the cheek and then she pulled on Jack's windbreaker for him to lean over toward her. He also received a kiss on the cheek.

The three of them beamed smiles from ear-to-ear. Rey's proselytizing had struck a nerve in both of them. But would this new found course of action become indelible or a simple fleeting moment.

CHAPTER 28

As usual, the temperature in El Cajon this date was predicted to hit 90 degrees. It was not unexpected, but it was dreaded by most of the residents. On North Mollison Avenue, Abdul planned one more of his rousing propaganda speeches and then he would disclose the final details regarding the event.

In the garage of the townhome, the five men assembled and found five folding chairs placed in a row. They knew that they were expected to sit down. Hanging from the far overhead door track were five suit bags, each with a small tag showing the numbers one through five.

All the men wore freshly ironed, dark-colored pants and white shirts. Two of them had been instructed earlier to wear ties which they would put on later in the day.

The men took their places and sat in silence. Rafid was antsy this day, looking at everything and nothing, wondering what he was doing there. Before he was able to become deep in thought, Abdul entered.

Abdul strode in like a general about to address his troops. He looked at the men with a blend of pride and disgust. He was proud that his rhetoric convinced these fools to give up their lives in exchange for a sweet payday for him. He was disgusted with his countrymen for being so stupid as to believe all his balderdash.

After Abdul assessed the crowd, it was Showtime.

"Gentlemen," he announced, "I must admit that I am envious of you and what you are about to undertake. Before the end of this day, you will all be in paradise. Greeted by both Muhammad and Allah, given a kiss on the cheek, and praised for your service."

The men did not react. They looked forward.

"You men know my name. Abdul Muhsi. Does anyone know what my name means?"

Silence enveloped the room. No one was willing to respond.

"It means 'Servant of the Reckoner.' That is exactly what you and I are today. A force of nature that cannot be stopped. A comeuppance to a great super power and a massive slaughter to a virulent pest.

"We are forced to engage in this jihad, because our enemy has enlisted the United States as their enforcer. They stand behind the United States and laugh at us like we were impotent fools. Their reputation is to get someone else to do their dirty work. It is time to punish the bully for their choices.

"We are going to bring terror to an area thought to be safe. America must learn that as long as they back this scourge, they will pay the price in blood. And our enemies must learn that there is a target on their backs and we will not rest until their existence is obliterated from the face of the earth.

"The goal of today's mission is volume. Both in number and in message – to resonate throughout the world. According to my calculations, the casualty list should exceed one thousand. And the history books, written by our historians, will record your names in awe and glory.

"Our goal is simple: to eradicate the world of the malignant and pernicious blight that vexes our very existence. I am speaking of the cancer known as the vile, common, gutter Jew."

Abdul scanned the group, knowing that in a few hours, their death sentence would be carried out. After that he would be able to focus on the money he received from Izzie the Fence. Until then, it was necessary to keep up the façade.

CHAPTER 29

Carol Ann Zelinsky began to believe that she was losing her grip on life. The only thing that she had eaten in the past 48 hours was a Snickers candy bar. She was experiencing cottonmouth and the muscles in her arms burned from being held up by handcuffs. Carol Ann had no idea what time it was until she heard the sliding of the three deadbolts.

The clothes were slid back and there stood Rory. He wore a different t-shirt, but his body odor was pungent. His hair looked greasy and his teeth were stained by recently eaten chocolate. In his hand was a Snickers bar. He ripped open one end and placed it in her right hand.

"Here," Rory told her. "I forgot to give this to you yesterday. I'm gonna go get my friend's truck. Then, you and I'll take a ride. Then, I'll let you go."

Carol Ann nodded with a brisk motion. Rory then flicked open his knife.

"Hold still."

He once again cut the duct tape, so she could eat the candy bar.

"I'm leaving as soon as you're done eating. I'm going to be right here in the kitchen. Don't get any cute ideas."

While Carol Ann ravenously scarfed the candy, Rory reached upwards to a high shelf in the kitchen to retrieve a bottle of chloroform. He set it on the counter with a rag. After that, he picked up the fish flakes and tapped a few shakes of it into the fish tank.

Rory moved the living room couch, chair, and coffee table off the rug in the center of the room. He grabbed some rope from a drawer and searched through several drawers before finding the final object: a weather-worn claw hammer.

Rory had a plan. Carol Ann now had less than one hour before the plan would go into motion and come to fruition.

CHAPTER 30

At Bergsteen Jewelers, located on Prospect Street in La Jolla, Izzie Bergsteen, also known as Izzie the Fence, was examining a two carat pear-shape diamond that he took in on consignment.

Izzie was famous for his attention to detail. Peering through his jeweler's eye loupe, he found two flaws: a slight crack that was barely noticeable and a chip out of the diamond. The chip was difficult to see because one of the prongs of the setting covered it.

The final item he always sought out was any laser inscription on the girdle of the diamond. This would allow him to trace the diamond if it was determined to be stolen. If there was no laser inscription, he could pass the information on to his criminal friends regarding the location of an expensive stone that could not be traced.

As his observation continued, his cell phone came to life. He looked at the Caller ID, but did not recognize the number.

"Hello," Izzie cautiously responded.

"Izzie, it's Wallace," answered the voice with a British accent.

"Who?"

"It's Ace," he replied in frustration.

"Your real name is Wallace?"

"Yeah."

"I never knew that."

"Me mum thought it was a good idea at the time. What's that situation with the key?"

Ace was hopeful that Izzie's inside person at the bank would be able to provide them with the bank key for the safe deposit box. One of Ace's confederates would then pick the lock for the renter's key within 30 seconds.

"The key will be there – under the mat. Don't rough up the mat."

Izzie was signaling to Ace that he did not want his inside person hurt.

"It's up to the mat how much it gets roughed up, mate. Time will be of the essence and I have no tolerance for heroism or showboating."

"When are you heading over there?" Izzie asked.

"You told me 3:30 was the other thing."

"Just checking."

"Don't worry. Start getting another suitcase ready. Cheerio, mate."

Ace was signaling Izzie to begin preparing the balance of the payment for the job. Izzie was feeling comfortable that the plans were coming together. The countdown to 3:30 pm was on.

CHAPTER 31

Rory's captive, Carol Ann Zelinsky, was revitalized by the Snickers candy bar Rory gave her. Earlier, she had cracked through the plasterboard wall that was covered by soundproof material. If she could break through the next wall, which she assumed was another piece of sheetrock or plasterboard, she might be able to get the attention of the next door neighbors.

Carol Ann grabbed the closet pole with both hands, although limited on the grip by the handcuffs, and started to swing using one foot to batter the wall. She would push off from the wall hoping for more momentum on the next swing into the wall.

Tillie Davenport and Levan Wentworth were the next door neighbors in Unit 5. They had been residents at the Agua Dulce Apartments for twenty-seven years. Tillie was 72 years old, African-American, and wore a red and white striped housedress. Levan was slightly older and heavyset. He had lost his foot to diabetes and was in the living room watching television.

"Levan. Levan," Tillie called out.

"What?" he yelled back.

"Call me when *Judge Judy* starts."

"What are you doing?" he asked.

"I'm taking my medicine."

"Hey, save a couple of hits for me."

Tillie was in the process of lighting a marijuana cigarette. She suffered from glaucoma and was able to purchase medical marijuana. Her attempts to ignite her Bic Lighter were unsuccessful.

"Levan, Levan," she wailed.

"WHAT?"

"Next time we go to Rite-Aid, we gotta get lighters."

"All right."

Tillie rose from her chair and started searching through a drawer for matches. It was then that she began to hear a thumping sound. She looked around wondering what the noise was. She then returned to her search.

The thumping continued. Tillie found an empty matchbook and then found a matchbook with matches. She returned to the kitchen table. As she began the process of lighting the cigarette, the thumping grew louder.

"Lord, a-mighty," she said quietly, "I hope that's not my heart."

Tillie placed her hand on her chest over her heart. She did not feel any irregularity.

"Levan!"

"Yeah?"

"Start a list for Rite-Aid. I also want to get some hearing aid batteries."

"Didn't we just get them?" Levan wondered.

"No. We didn't like the expiration date."

Just as Tillie finished her sentence, a portion of the kitchen wall cracked.

"OH, LORD JESUS!" Tillie screamed. "I hope it's not rats."

With the next swing, the heel of Carol Ann's foot came through the wallpaper. She pulled her foot back and stopped swinging.

Tillie slowly approached the ripped wallpaper and pulled it back and looked inside. She heard a muffled sound and picked up a flashlight off the table. Tillie turned it on and peered into the closet. There was Carol Ann with wide eyes of terror.

"LEVAN! LEVAN!"

"What is going on in there, woman? Don't tell me that weed is bad. That guy told me it was premium."

"There's a white girl next door, tied up. She's trying to come through the wall. Call the nine-one-one."

"*Judge Judy* is about to start," Levan mentioned.

"Call the Po-leese. We gotta help this girl."

Carol Ann was about to be freed and Rory was about to become a fugitive.

CHAPTER 32

Jack stared at the telephone in his cubicle and assessed his next course of action. He called the FBI three times and either hung up or told them it was the wrong number. For some reason, he was paralyzed by fear. Jack would not call them now because he thought they would trace the calls back to the dealership.

Maybe Abdul was just an immigrant with a dog business on the side. Or maybe he was a terrorist plotting extraordinary bloodshed. Jack weighed this against Rey's comments that the only thing necessary for the triumph of evil is that good men do nothing.

The conflict within Jack was tearing him apart. It captivated his mind and preoccupied his every thought. He wondered why he even cared. Every time he decided to ignore it, the situation ascended to the front of his mind placing him in what looked like a catatonic state.

The telephone rang to break the silence.

"Thunderbar Buick. This is Jack."

"Jack, it's Smitty. I'm down in Mission Valley. Are there any other parts orders before I head back up there?"

"Hold on."

Jack checked the tally sheet and all the orders were filled.

"Looks like you got them all, Smitty. You might as well head back up here."

"Jack, I'll take the afternoon runs for the courtesy shuttle. If you have something to do, take the afternoon off."

"Thanks, Smitty, maybe I will. I'll see you later."

"Take care."

With that, the call ended. Jack returned the receiver to its cradle. He went into deep thought, looking forward without focus.

"Jack. Jack. JACK!"

It was Bill Godfrey, the Customer Service Manager at the dealership, standing at the entrance to Jack's cubicle.

"Yeah, Bill?" Jack asked as he regained his composure.

"Is everything okay?"

"Yeah."

"You seem a little distant."

"Can I take the afternoon off? I've got something I have to do."

"Sure," Bill told him.

"I'll be here tomorrow," Jack said, but for some reason his voice had an air of finality.

"Any problems, just call."

"Okay, thanks."

Jack closed his computer programs. He left the dealership and walked briskly to his car. If any insidious action was going to happen this day, Jack would attempt to stop it. He wanted to bring one thing with him before heading off to the Jewish Academy and it was located in his apartment.

The time was 1:30 pm. Jack was planning on a showdown, if necessary. He did not know what he was about to do, but he was sure that he was about to find out Abdul's true intentions.

CHAPTER 33

At the 76 gas station, located at 1202 South Coast Highway, regular gasoline was selling for $2.83 a gallon. The station was located within two blocks of the Laundromat Lounge and ten blocks from the Dolphin Hotel.

Rory pulled into the station driving a tan, 1974 Chevy 1500 pickup truck. It was badly battered and severely rusted around the wheel wells, but the bed of the truck was eight feet long and sound.

The bed of the truck was empty with the exception of a long-handled, digging shovel that Rory borrowed from his friend, Zee. Rory had promised Zee that he would put some gas in the truck before he returned it to him.

The truck had less than one-quarter of a tank of gas. Rory retrieved his wallet out from his backpack and walked inside the station. He paid for twenty dollars of gas on the pump closest to the truck. Rory returned to the passenger side of the truck, opened the door, and grabbed his backpack from the floor of the cab.

Rory then saw something that caught his eye. He saw a bit of black metal jutting out from under the seat. He reached for it and it was a Colt 1911 .45 caliber semi-automatic pistol.

It was surprisingly heavy in his hand. Rory held it in his hand and dropped the magazine out of it to see that it was fully loaded. He pulled the slide back on the gun and observed a bullet in the chamber. Rory replaced the clip into the gun and placed it into his backpack.

He proceeded to pump eighteen dollars worth of gas into the truck. His plan was to use the two dollars of change for either candy or chips.

Rory went back inside the station, grabbed a small package of Cheetos and got in line behind five other customers. As he stood there, the local news played on a large screen television that hung on the wall. The following story began:

> A missing Oceanside woman was found safe today after being kidnapped and held prisoner for nearly three days in a closet of an apartment building on South Ditmar Street. Carol Ann Zelinsky was abducted on Monday night as she walked home from class at the Oceanside College of Beauty. Ms. Zelinsky was hospitalized and is currently in stable condition. Police are now searching for the resident of the apartment, Rory Dahl, who is considered a suspect in the abduction. Mr. Dahl carries a knife and should be considered extremely dangerous. Anyone with information on his whereabouts is asked to call the Oceanside Police Department or Crime Stoppers.

When Rory's name was mentioned, his driver's license picture appeared on the screen. As soon as the news report ended, he made a beeline out the door, without his change, and directly to the truck.

Rory needed a new plan and he needed one fast.

CHAPTER 34

The temperature continued to rise in El Cajon. At the North Mollison townhome of Abdul Muhsi, Abdul prepared for his final, yet most important, speech.

The five suicide bombers gathered in Abdul's garage and awaited their Emir, or leader. They were dressed in suit pants, white shirts, and two of them wore nondescript ties. Abdul entered the garage, carrying one visual aid. He scanned the group before starting to speak.

"Gentlemen, today you will make history. Not only for what you are about to carry out, but in terms of a scientific breakthrough that will slap America in its face and leave them scratching their heads as to how to stop it. Fear and blood will run in the streets unabated."

There was no response from any of the men. Abdul continued.

"You are all going to wear finely-tailored suit coats that have been created specifically for you. These custom coats will contain a liner that makes them slightly heavier than a traditional suit coat. Contained within the liner is a plastic explosive, known as Octanitrocubane or Octy. When Octy is mixed with a plasticizer it becomes a solid explosive, like TNT. But let me share some distinct differences.

"TNT has a detonation speed of 6,000 meters per second. Octy has a detonation speed of 10,600 meters per second. It is considered approximately 2.38 times more powerful than TNT. The United States government keeps this explosive under heavy guard. We now have access to it.

"In addition, the explosive lining of your jackets have been saturated with the plasticizer and with a compound called hydrogen cyanide. Upon detonation, the hydrogen cyanide becomes aerosolized or broken up into little droplets. Inhalation will be fatal in less than one minute.

"If the explosion does not kill them, the air will. As for each of you, there is no concern. Your proximity to the detonation site indicates that you will be vaporized in less than a second. Any questions?"

Rafid raised his hand and Abdul pointed to him.

"So, this explosive has not been tested before?

"Not at this level, but it has been tested."

"So, how do you know that it is going to work?" Rafid wondered.

"I'll discuss it with you when we are done here," Abdul acknowledged with a perturbed smirk. "All right?"

"Yes," Rafid replied.

"Now, the actual event. The speech is set to take place in the school's gymnasium. It will be standing room only. The speech will also be broadcast to two off-site locations: the auditorium or theater and the cafeteria. In the pocket of your suit coat, you will find the area to which you are assigned."

Abdul then revealed his visual aid. It was a schematic drawing of the auditorium and the two off-site locations. On each drawing there were concentric circles.

"These circles," Abdul pointed, "represent the blast zone and the kill zone. The power of the blast is lessened as it moves farther away from the point of detonation. Therefore, it is necessary for you not to be against a wall, but more toward the center of the room. One of you will be sent to the front of the gymnasium close to the speaker. This is to ensure his death. Any questions?"

No one responded.

"I will drop you off at the school. Once you exit the car – disperse. Don't stand near each other. Head to your destinations.

"The final piece of information is that also in your pockets is a very small transmitter. When you believe that you have located an area that offers the maximum kill zone range, push the button on the transmitter. Once everyone is in place, the explosives will be detonated. Do not yell '*Allah Akbar*' because we do not want to give anyone advance notice of our intentions. For the final time, any questions?"

There were no questions.

"If anyone has to go to the bathroom, take care of it now. If you are thirsty, get a drink. If anyone would like a piece of gum, let me know."

One man raised his hand. Abdul reached in his pocket and pulled out a pack of Juicy Fruit gum. He tossed the pack to him and turned his attention to Rafid.

"Rafid, I would like to speak to you. Upstairs."

Rafid followed Abdul to the living room of the main floor.

"Why are you trying to undermine this effort?" Abdul inquired.

"I don't know what you are talking about."

"Inherent in your question is the risk of failure. If that happens, you will all go to the American jail for pigs."

"I," Rafid retorted, "am putting my life in service to this cause. I think I should be allowed to ask such a simple question."

"I consider you to be the most zealous warrior of the group. You will be in charge of the detonator. You can set it off at any time. You do not have to hear back from all of them. Now, is when I need you to be the strongest. Understood?"

Rafid nodded.

"*Allah Akbar*," Abdul told him.

"*Allah Akbar*," Rafid replied.

In less than thirty minutes, the car ride to their destination would commence.

CHAPTER 35

At 3:00 pm, Ace walked out of the office at Bud's British Import into the garage area. Baz, Rick and Reggie were waiting for him at the far end of the garage, away from the showroom area. All the men wore British Overcoats that covered a bulletproof vest. Reggie had boosted, or stolen, three cars. The cars included a Dodge Challenger, Dodge Charger, and Chevrolet Corvette. All had HEMI engines that put out nearly 400 horsepower of speed.

"All right, boys," Ace began. "Wheels up. Baz – pass out the artillery. Rick – what are we wearin' for face masks?"

Baz passed out a Glock 9mm handgun to Ace, Reggie and Rick. For himself, he would have a modified 12-gauge Mossberg Compact Cruiser shotgun with an eight-inch barrel. This was a short, tactical shotgun, easy to conceal under his coat, and guaranteed to terrorize anyone who saw it in action.

"I got us skull kerchiefs to cover the bottom of our faces," Rick advised as he handed out the items. "You," referring to Ace, "get a Fedora for a hat and we wear ski hats to cover the top. We all get a pair of sunglasses. Maximum visibility. Minimum recognition."

"Remember," Ace advised, "keep conversation to a minimum. If necessary, try an American accent and no British slang."

"Time to boogie?" Reggie inquired.

Ace shook his head affirmatively.

"God save the Queen," Reggie added.

"Ace," Baz interjected just as the men started to move. "If we end up going *mano-a-mano* with the rozzers (police), do we settle it right then and there? Blood on the dancefloor?"

"This job is not worth dying for. And we already got seventy-five percent of the payday. Anybody gets pinched, we're going to sell out our friend, Izzie the Fence. We got him on video. As for us, worst case, we get bailed out and go on a long vacation."

"You know, I'm not going to do time," Baz warned.

"There's nothing to worry about," Ace told him while giving him a slight tap on the cheek. "This one is going to be a walk in the park. Let's hit it."

Ace and Reggie got into the Dodge Challenger with Reggie driving.

"Reg, keep an ear on the police band. We should be in and out fast. You hear anything about a 2-11 in progress, let me know."

"Done," Reggie acknowledged.

The caravan of vehicles, led by Ace, were on their way to Sunset Savings in La Jolla. The plan was in motion.

CHAPTER 36

Jack was able to find a parking space right by the entrance to the Dolphin Hotel on West Topeka Avenue. He darted from his car into the lobby, just in time to see Flip take his usual perch behind the reception counter. Flip wore the same sweater and pants, but today he wore a light green button shirt.

"Afternoon, Mr. Jack," he uttered with a smile.

"Hello, Flip, how are you today?"

"Today, I decided I'm gonna finish my book."

"*Slaughterhouse 5*," Jack said while pointing his finger at him.

"Good memory."

"Listen," Jack told him, "I have to get going. We'll talk later."

Jack turned to walk away and Flip spoke up.

"Hey, Mr. Jack, your mailbox is overflowing. Can you grab your mail?"

Jack stepped behind the counter and yanked his mail out of the slot with his name and apartment number.

"There's also a letter there for Miss Rey, if you want to bring it to her."

Jack grabbed Rey's letter and placed it on his pile of mail. He scurried up the stairs and into his apartment. Jack took off his windbreaker and threw it on the bed. He then opened one of the cabinet doors over the microwave and reached up to the top shelf. Jack pulled out a Smith & Wesson, M & P .40 caliber semi-automatic handgun.

He dropped the magazine out of the gun to make sure it was fully loaded. He then pulled back the slide on the gun to make sure a bullet was ready to be fired.

Jack placed the pistol on the counter and leaned against it. Jack took a deep breath and let it out. When he exhaled, he looked at the stack of mail and saw the letter to Rey. He froze. Something had shocked him. His head slowly raised and his mind was trying to figure something out. The wheels in his brain were now red hot on fire.

Jack looked at the letter one more time and, for a moment, did not know what to do next.

He picked up the gun and tucked it in his belt behind his back. Jack grabbed his windbreaker off the bed and put it on as he moved to the door.

Outside of his apartment door, he locked it and turned. There stood Rey.

Their eyes locked. Rey had a stern visage and Jack was surprised to see her. Rey held out her hand to him, palm up.

"Give me the gun."

Jack continued to stare at her.

"No. I know who you are."

"Then, I hope you'll listen to me. You have good intentions, but you're going about it the wrong way. If you bring that gun, you will give them an excuse to kill you. You said you live in darkness, the absence of light. Now, I want you to walk by faith, not by what your eyes tell you."

"What are you doing here?"

"You need me. Sophie needs me. I go where I'm needed."

"I have to stop them, Rey."

"Is that what you want?" Rey's voice raised. "To be a faceless martyr, who's forgotten in 48 hours? Your family does not want you to die today. You have been given a gift by God and it is up to you to figure out how to use it."

Jack contemplated what she said.

"I can't stand by and let them kill all those people."

"You've got the make and model of the car and the license plate number. Call the Highway Patrol and let them take care of it."

"So, I should stay here and do nothing?" Jack asked in desperation.

"No," she answered succinctly. "There's a bank on Torrey Pines Road in La Jolla. Sunset Savings. It's about to be robbed in thirty minutes. Go there and stop that robbery."

"How?" Jack wondered.

"You have to figure it out."

Jack gazed upon Rey and reached for the gun tucked in his belt. He handed the gun to Rey, grip first.

"Why did my family have to die that day?"

"So that you would be standing right here, right now, at this point in time."

Jack was trying to comprehend what she said.

"Goodbye, Rey," he told her.

"Goodbye, Jack."

Jack raced out of the Dolphin Hotel directly to his Honda Accord with La Jolla as his destination. He had an appointment with destiny.

CHAPTER 37

While Jack scrambled to La Jolla, Abdul and his men loaded into Abdul's 1996 Buick Roadmaster station wagon. One man sat in the passenger seat, three in the back seat, and Rafid sat in a seat that was in the cargo area, which faced the other way. All the men wore their suicide suit coats. The coats were stiff, but onlookers would not notice a difference.

Not a word was spoken in the vehicle as it entered the freeway for a thirty minute drive to the Jewish Academy. Traffic was light and Abdul made sure that he drove along with the traffic and did not exceed the speed limit.

Approximately fifteen minutes into the ride, they approached the ramp from Interstate 8 to Interstate 805. Abdul noticed a California Highway Patrol cruiser behind him and did not want to bring any attention to his car. As Abdul drove up the ramp, the CHP car followed. He merged into the traffic on Interstate 805 and the red and blue emergency lights on the top of the vehicle turned on.

Abdul pulled over to the side of the road. He sat looking forward.

"No one speak. I'll handle this."

The police cruiser was a late model Ford Expedition. This vehicle was equipped with a Police Intervention Technique, or PIT, bumper and had ballistic protection from small arms fire.

Jack had called the CHP and advised them that Abdul's vehicle may be involved in some sort of terrorist activity. The CHP issued a BOLO, or 'be on the lookout,' for the vehicle.

Officer Anthony Guerro called in the plate number to the CHP dispatch center and was advised that there were no wants or warrants for the car. He stepped out of the vehicle and approached the Buick Roadmaster. Abdul rolled down his window as he arrived.

"Good afternoon, Officer. Is there a problem?"

"Can I see your license, registration, and proof of insurance?"

"Certainly."

Abdul complied.

"I would like to know why you stopped me."

"We had a report this car may be involved in some criminal activity."

"That's preposterous. I'm a history professor at the community college in El Cajon. These men are students and we are going to a lecture."

Officer Guerro looked at the other passengers. They all either looked out the window or directly at him and smiled.

"All right. I'll be right back."

The officer walked back to his police vehicle.

"We should take off and make a run for it. We can still achieve our objective," Rafid said without turning his head.

"No," Abdul replied. "They would have police up ahead to stop us. I can talk my way out of this."

A second CHP vehicle pulled up and parked behind Officer Guerro. This car was also a Ford Expedition driven by an Officer Phillip Rodriguez.

Rodriguez walked up to Guerro's car and sat in the passenger seat.

"What do we got, Tony?" Rodriguez wondered.

"I don't know. There was a BOLO issued for this car and the driver and the car are coming back clean. I think the guys in the car are acting kind of squirrelly."

"What do you want to do?" Rodriguez asked.

Officer Guerro decided not to take any chances.

"Call dispatch," he told Rodriguez, "tell them we stopped the car and it's occupied six times. Tell them to start two cars for us and tell them to step it up. You and I can start pulling them out of the vehicle."

Rodriguez called it in. Both officers stepped out of the car and stood between their open door and the car. They both upholstered their service weapons and took a firing stance at the vehicle. Guerro spoke through the loudspeaker on his vehicle.

"DRIVER! Let me see both hands outside the window."

Abdul complied.

"With your right hand, open the door!"

Abdul went to reach for the door handle when Rafid interrupted the silence within the vehicle.

"STOP! Don't do it. Roll up the window."

Abdul brought his hands in and rolled up the window.

"Let me go talk to them," Abdul persisted. "I can talk our way out of this."

"Time for talk is over," Rafid announced. "Let them come to us."

"You want to kill two police officers instead of a thousand Jews?"

"I want to do both. We can use this car as a suicide bomb. We'll drive right into the crowd."

"Then let me out," Abdul pleaded. "I'm much more valuable here for recruitment."

"No," Rafid assured him with his words coming out slowly. "Today, Servant of the Reckoner, we can all meet Allah together and celebrate our labors."

Abdul started to open his door when Rafid turned around holding the detonator for the suit coats.

"You open that door and I'll detonate the bombs. You don't practice what you preach. Your words are like zeros on a piece of paper. They mean nothing."

Two additional CHP vehicles arrived at the scene. A CHP helicopter could be heard in the distance.

"Rafid," Abdul commanded, "let me out of this vehicle!"

"After you answer one question: Where did you get all that money that's in your closet? I found it yesterday when you went to get food."

Abdul was shocked but thought quickly.

"It's for another project, based on the success of this one."

Rafid laughed for a moment and looked at the men, who stared at him. He turned around and sat back in his seat.

"A liar is like a magician. They are both good at making the truth disappear."

A moment passed. Then Rafid made a final comment in a quiet voice.

"*Allah Akbar*," he uttered and detonated the vests.

A cataclysmic explosion erupted within the vehicle. All the doors shot off the car like high-powered bullets. The roof of the station wagon ripped open leaving jagged metal around the open hole.

The supersonic shockwave of fire and energy raged out like a blast furnace from the roasted shell of the car. Fire roared out as if it was coming from a jet engine. A concentric circle of energy pulsed out at lightning speed breaking all glass it touched and knocking down anything that was not securely attached to the ground.

The two CHP officers had no time to react. The explosion broke all the glass on all four CHP cruisers. It lifted the front end of Guerro's police car and nearly flipped it over. The front of the car raised six feet off the ground after being pushed back ten feet into the next cruiser and dropped.

The two officers were slammed by Guerro's car and car door down to the pavement. They were in critical condition. Both were unconscious and from their ears ran a combination of pus, wax, fluid and blood. Their eardrums were ruptured.

Any vehicle within two miles of the detonation site felt the power of the blast. The CHP helicopter was hit by the turbulence and quickly moved to a safer location.

All six men within the vehicle were vaporized. The blast was so powerful and so hot that the hydrogen cyanide soaked into the plastic explosive also vaporized. It never made it into the air.

The car continued to burn for three hours. Water had no effect on it. The temperature, at one point, reached two thousand degrees Fahrenheit. Eventually, the car totally melted along with Abdul's hatred, bigotry, and blind followers.

CHAPTER 38

Ten minutes earlier, Ace and his men pulled into the parking lot of Sunset Savings on Torrey Pines Road in La Jolla. There were few other cars in the lot. They parked their three cars next to each other facing toward the exit for a quicker getaway.

The three men pulled their kerchiefs up above their noses and exited the vehicles. They walked toward the bank, looking down as if they were coughing. This was to conceal the skull on their kerchief and to minimize any attention in the event someone was watching the video feed. Reggie stayed in the Dodge Challenger to act as a lookout and to monitor the police radio band.

As soon as they entered the bank, Ace walked up to the lone security guard, a 68-year-old retired San Diego County Sheriff's deputy, and put his 9mm Glock handgun behind the guard's ear before the guard even noticed him.

"Don't move," Ace told him. "Left hand. Remove the gun."

The security guard's eyes opened wide. He took the safety off his holster and handed the gun to Ace.

"Lift your trouser leg. Both of them."

The security guard complied and Ace was satisfied that he did not have an ankle gun.

"Get down on the floor," Ace commanded.

Ace signaled to Rick, who placed zip tie restraints on him.

When you entered the bank, there was a row of teller windows on the left side and eight desks on the right side to allow customers to open accounts and discuss matters with bank personnel.

While Ace was dealing with the security guard, Baz began to deal with the three tellers, two customers, and four management people. He swept the shotgun back and forth across the room. Everyone froze. Ace moved in with fluid precision.

"Tellers, step back from the cash drawers. Come on this side of the windows. Everybody on the ground."

The tellers walked slowly around and complied. Rick proceeded to place zip ties on all three tellers. Right before he did this, Rick placed three zip ties on the inside handles of the entrance doors to the bank. No one could come in from the outside.

"You people," Ace ordered, referring to the management people, "I need the bank key for the safe deposit boxes. Now!"

None of the four management people moved. Ace knew from Izzie that the inside person's name was Jane. There were two male management people. Ace called over the two men.

"You and you," he pointed and directed them to him. Rick proceed to place zip ties on them and put them on the floor.

Ace sped over to one of the remaining two women. She had long blonde hair. He grabbed it and wrapped it tight in his left hand. That is when Ace realized something that Izzie did not tell him. On each desk, there was a nameplate. Both of these women were named Jane.

"Do you have the key?" he quizzed the woman as he pulled her hair.

"No, she has it," she answered through frightened pain.

Ace then pointed the gun at the other Jane.

"Give me the key or I'm going to shoot her."

"I don't have it. She has it."

"I'll take it off your corpse."

Ace put the gun up to the first Jane's temple when a voice from one of the customers interrupted the conversation.

"The one you're holding doesn't have it. The other one does."

They all looked to see who was speaking. It was Jack.

Ace let go of the first Jane and called the other Jane over. She produced the key.

Ace swiftly handed the key to Rick, who moved to the safe deposit box room to begin picking the lock on box number 286.

"Put zip ties on the customers," Ace told Baz.

Baz rapidly placed them on the female customer. Then Ace received some news through an earpiece he was wearing.

"The call just went out," Reggie shared. "Two-eleven in progress."

Rick came out of the safe deposit room holding the Chase & Sanborn coffee can. As promised, the lock was picked within thirty seconds.

Ace took the can and moved toward the Jane that had the key. He pushed her back to the wall behind her desk.

"Next time do what you're told or you are going to take a bullet."

Ace acted as if he was moving the coffee can within his coat. He went down on one knee and placed the can next to a large Michael Kors purse that was under the desk.

"Let's go," Ace commanded and the men were in motion.

Baz never placed a zip tie on Jack. In the midst of all the action, Baz was not paying attention. Rick cut the zip ties off the door and was in his car driving south within seconds. Baz was in his car immediately and heading north. Reggie's car was running and waiting for Ace.

Just as Ace hit the bank's entrance doors, Jack tackled him from behind. They scuffled for a moment, but Ace quickly had the advantage. He pinned Jack down and put the gun to his head.

"It's not worth it," Ace told him.

The men stared at each other.

"Pull the trigger," Jack told him. "Do it."

The sound of sirens were now filling the air. Reggie, Ace's getaway driver, took off.

Ace stood up, dropped the gun, and brushed off his coat. The parking lot was filling with police vehicles. Ace had a question for Jack.

"How did you know that girl had the key?"

"It was the look in her face," Jack answered.

When Jack first entered the bank, he scanned the faces of everyone inside. That Jane, who ultimately gave up the key, was the only face on which he saw an x-ray of a skull.

CHAPTER 39

Sophie's day at the Laundromat Lounge was uneventful. When 7:00 pm rolled around, she closed all the lights and waited for Jack. He was debriefed by the San Diego Police and an FBI special agent. Now, the late rush hour traffic was slowing his return to Oceanside.

After ten minutes, Sophie decided that she would walk back to the Dolphin Hotel. She locked the door and began her trek. When Sophie crossed the second block of South Coast Highway, Jack pulled up alongside of her. He waved her into the vehicle.

"Sorry, I'm late," Jack told her.

"It's all right. I figured you were busy."

"How was your day?" Jack asked.

"Pretty quiet. How 'bout yours?" Sophie wondered.

"Interesting. I'll tell you and Rey about it when we get back."

Sophie looked out the window as she asked her next question.

"Do you ever miss being a lawyer?"

"No," Jack answered succinctly. "There were too many painful memories. Did you have a career that you were thinking about going after?"

"A teacher. Maybe a nurse."

"You would be good at either one."

Jack reached the corner of West Topeka and South Coast Highway. He turned down West Topeka Street and found a parking space midway down the block.

Jack and Sophie hiked down to the entrance to the Dolphin Hotel. They walked in and Flip was still reading *Slaughterhouse 5*.

"Flip, how's that book coming along?" Jack inquired, breaking Flip's concentration.

"I got a couple, three chapters left. Evening, Miss Sophie."

"Good evening, Flip. Did you have a good day?"

"Well, I'm still above the ground. So, I'd say, yeah, I had a good day." Flip's smile beamed.

Sophie ascended the staircase to the second floor followed by Jack. Each proceeded to the door of their apartment.

"I'll see you shortly, Sophie."

Jack walked into his room, took off his windbreaker, and tossed it on the bed. He loosened his tie and flipped on a light switch. Turning on the light was never part of his normal routine.

Light flooded the barren room. He decided that he wanted to share the day's experiences with Rey.

Jack headed to Rey's room and knocked on the door. There was no answer. He turned the knob on the door and it was unlocked. Jack stepped into the room and turned on a light immediately.

Moments earlier, Sophie entered her apartment, turned on the light, and walked straight in to look out the window. The light brightened a black shadow in her bathroom. The shadow took the shape of a man and walked out of the bathroom toward Sophie as she peered out the window. It was Rory.

Jack had entered Rey's apartment and it was empty. All of Rey's possessions were gone. The counter, where the microwave once sat, was empty except for three items, piled on top of each other. The top item was a small rosary that was handmade out of wooden beads. The second item was Jack's Smith & Wesson, M & P .40 caliber semi-automatic handgun. The third item was a yellow Post-it note. It read:

Jack,

Help Sophie!

Love,

Rey

As soon as he read the note, he heard Sophie scream and yell for help. Jack grabbed his gun and ran to Sophie's door. He clicked off the safety on the gun and tried the door handle. The door was locked.

Jack lifted his foot and smashed it into the center of the door. The lock ruptured and the door flew open. As it swung open, Rory fired two shots out the door with his .45 caliber Colt handgun.

Jack fell back on his butt. As he was falling, he fired one round without aiming. Jack then rolled to the side of the door that opens and stood up, with his gun pointed to the ceiling.

"Hey grandpa! I hope those gunshots don't bother your hearing aids. Shouldn't you be at an early bird special?"

Downstairs, Flip was startled by the sound of gunfire. He crouched down to take cover under the desk. He reached his hand up and grabbed the receiver of the telephone on his desk. He dialed nine-one-one.

"I'm not going to let you walk out with her," Jack shouted.

"Why do you want to save this tramp? Ask her how she used to make a living before she learned how to Fluff & Fold. You couldn't save your family. What makes you think you can save her?"

Rory stood there calmly with a grin of evil and the gun pointed to Sophie's head.

"What were you doing that day, Jack? The day your family died. You forgot that part of the story. Remember your saying: Successful men have two of everything – houses, cars, women."

"SHUTUP!" Jack screamed. "Satan, I rebuke you in the name of Christ the Redeemer!"

There was a moment of silence. Then, a short, insidious laugh.

"Sorry, Jack, it doesn't work that way. Without action, they're just words. I guess that old lady didn't tell you that. Makes you wonder what else she didn't tell you. Let me outta here and I'll tell you the real reason why your family had to die that day."

"Don't listen to him, Jack. He's going to lie to you," Sophie pleaded.

Jack thought for a moment about what was going on. He was done with the mental judo that was being played. Jack moved to the doorway and looked at Rory and Sophie. Rory's face turned to an x-ray, but this time it lasted more than just a quick moment.

Jack let go of his gun and it dropped to the floor.

"Kill me," Jack told him.

Rory peered at him with a villainous chagrin.

"Come on! Do it!" Jack demanded. "KILL ME!"

Rory slowly moved the gun from Sophie's head. He stretched out his arm and took aim at Jack. As the gun was about to be leveled, Sophie sprang into action.

"Noooooo!" she screamed.

She pushed the gun away and Rory fired it once. The recoil of the gun threw Rory off balance. He let go of Sophie, but also pistol-whipped her in the face. The impact knocked her to the ground.

Jack charged at Rory and they struggled for Rory's gun. Rory fired the gun, hoping its kick would break Jack's grip. It did not. The second shot caused Jack to let go of Rory's wrist.

As soon as Jack let go of his wrist, Rory bolted out the door. Jack was in hot pursuit, as he had picked up his gun on the way out of Sophie's apartment.

Rory reached the top of the stairs, still moving at full speed and looked back to see if he was being followed. As he looked, he stepped on one of his untied shoelaces.

Rory tumbled down the stairs and hurriedly rolled to the bottom of the staircase, still holding his handgun.

"FREEZE!"

Rory started to slowly turn and moved to all fours. There stood six Oceanside Police SWAT officers. Three were standing and three were kneeling in front of the standing officers, like a firing squad awaiting the order to deliver justice.

They were dressed in black, wearing body armor, and helmets that concealed their faces. They looked like robots, with an intimidating presence, lacking any human sympathy. They each carried a Heckler & Koch, .45 caliber UMP submachine gun. All six of them were now aimed at Rory.

"TOSS THE GUN OVER HERE!" the same voice commanded.

Rory looked at them and commenced the same diabolical laugh that he used earlier with Jack. Rory sprung and moved the gun in the direction of the SWAT officers.

The machine guns came to life and viciously pumped out hollow point bullets that ripped Rory apart.

"CEASE FIRE!" was called out.

The bullets stopped firing after three seconds. Light, white smoke wafted from the end of the gun barrels, which were still trained on Rory. The smell of gun smoke filled the air. There were 180 bullets fired and 167 struck Rory.

Jack watched all of the action from the top of the staircase. He turned and saw Sophie leaning against one of the hallway walls. She was cut and badly bruised on the cheek. The blood from her cut was running down her cheek and onto her shirt. Jack hurried over to her and smiled. They shared a quick, tight hug.

"Is it over?" she asked.

"Yeah," he answered.

"Are we still going to dinner together?" Sophie wondered. "Where's Rey?"

CHAPTER 40

The police spoke to both Jack and Sophie until well past midnight. The next day, both of them took the day off from work. Jack decided to make good on his promise and took Sophie out to lunch. They went to Angelo's Burgers, located eight blocks from the Dolphin Hotel on South Coast Highway in Oceanside.

Angelo's Burgers had a reputation for great food, large portions, and excellent prices. In addition to burgers, they were famous for their Greek food, Mexican food, French fries and onion rings. The interior had a red and white décor and was filled with booths. People were coming and going, but to Jack and Sophie, they seemed to be the only ones in the restaurant.

As they waited for their food order number to be called, they sat in a booth near the window with uncomfortable smiles. Sophie had a large bandage on her swollen cheek and a black eye. When Jack told her, the night before, that Rey was gone, she was hysterical. Jack was not going to broach the subject, but Sophie did.

"Why would she leave without saying goodbye?" Sophie wondered in amazement.

"Did you know what Rey's name was? Her full name?" Jack inquired.

Sophie contemplated his question.

"No. Reyna something?"

"Reyna D. Himmel."

"Okay. So?" Sophie quizzed.

"Reyna in Spanish means 'queen.'" Himmel in German means 'heaven.'"

"Queen of heaven," Sophie answered matter-of-factly.

Jack simply looked at her.

"You think that Rey was the Blessed Mother? The Virgin Mary?"

"Yep."

"What makes you say that?"

"She pretty much told me earlier in the day yesterday. Think back over the past three days. It makes sense," Jack shared.

Sophie became pensive. She then looked at Jack.

"The Mother of Jesus knitted me this sweater," Sophie uttered in astonishment.

"She cooked for us and made us cookies and iced tea."

"Why do you think she did her name in the Spanish and the German?" she wondered.

"Because I took a year of Spanish in high school and a year of German in college," Jack told her.

Then, their number was called indicating their food was ready for pick up. Jack started to slide out of the booth when Sophie grabbed one of his hands.

"Do you think you could help me get back to my parents in Indiana? I don't know if they want to see me, but I'd like to try."

"Absolutely," he answered definitely. "You know if my daughter was alive, she'd be the same age as you."

"So, if I need a dad, would you help me out?"

"You don't have to ask twice."

Jack picked up her hand and kissed the back of it. He then proceeded to the counter to pick up their food.

CHAPTER 41

As for the robbery crew, Baz, Rick, and Reggie were able to evade the police without notice. Ace was working on a plea bargain that did not include the names of any of his confederates. He did not disclose to the district attorney any information about the involvement of Izzie the Fence, but he indicated that the robbery was part of an intricate plan that might include the explosion that took place on Interstate 15.

When Izzie found out that both the bombing and the robbery were foiled, he was incensed. He wanted his money back.

He had one of his employees do nothing else but continually call Abdul's house with no success. Izzie visited the house with the thought of breaking in. He was dissuaded by a sticker in the corner of one of the windows indicating that the home was monitored by a security company. Abdul did not set the alarm when he left. The money sat in Abdul's closet.

As for Ace, Izzie would not speak to him for fear of association. Izzie went to Bud's British Import and spoke to Baz. Izzie demanded the return of the money and Baz feigned ignorance as to the location of the money. Baz asked Izzie for the $175,000 owed for the balance of the job. Izzie became infuriated and threatened to 'drop a dime' on the whole crew at Bud's British Import.

Izzie's body was found two days later, along with the inside bank person, Jane, in a darkened parking lot of a shopping center in La Jolla. Both were shot in the head. All Izzie's wife knew was that he was going to pick something up.

On the showroom floor of Bud's British Import, sat Izzie's red Bentley, complete with the title and registration signed over to them. The sale price was $175,000.

EPILOGUE
41 YEARS LATER

The La Costa Glen retirement community in Carlsbad, California provided assisted living care, Alzheimer's care, and long-term, skilled nursing care. Residents raved about the cleanliness of the facility, the kindness of the employees, and the food. The care was personalized for the needs of each resident.

In the skilled nursing care area, Jack laid in a bed that looked more like a hyperbaric chamber. He was encased inside a rounded, glass dome that allowed him to be in an area that was decontaminated from germs, bacteria, and dust. Pure oxygen was pumped in to allow maximum breathing potential. All the residents in this area, who were not ambulatory, reposed in one of these devices.

Jack had been bedridden for the past five years. His knees and hips had weakened and his heart had become more debilitated in the last several months. His head was elevated, so he could see out the window. The sun made everything it shone upon more vibrant.

Jack never married again after those three days. Instead, he spent his time in service to the church. Whenever he saw an x-ray on a face, he would take out a small vial of holy water and place a drop on the index finger on his left hand. Then he would rub it onto his thumb and middle finger. Jack would walk directly up to the person, no matter what they were doing, and immediately place his thumb and middle finger on each temple and his index finger at the top of the person's forehead. He would then say to them in a quiet voice, but loud enough to be sure they heard: 'Satan, I rebuke you in the name of Christ the Redeemer!'

The person would collapse as if under a hypnotist's spell for a quick moment and then revive. Jack would then say: 'I'll see you in Church. You need to go.'

Jack figured that in the past forty years, he had done this service more than a thousand times.

He stayed in touch with Sophie as much as he could. Once he became bedridden, that stopped.

As Jack reflected on the past, his concentration was interrupted by a chime indicating a message from the Nurse's Station.

"Yes," Jack answered.

"Mr. Vance, you have a visitor."

Jack continued to look out the window and could not imagine who would come to visit. Most of his friends were now dead and the staff would not be announced as a visitor.

Suddenly, there was a tap on the glass that surrounded Jack. Jack turned and it was as if he was re-born. His mouth was open and he reached over to open the glass housing.

As it opened, his visitor started to speak.

"Hello, Jack."

"Hello, Rey," he said with warm enthusiasm.

There stood Rey. She had not aged one day since those three days that occurred forty-one years earlier. She wore the exact same clothing down to the pill box hat with a piece of French veil.

"How are you?" she asked.

"Wonderful now," he exclaimed. "I have missed you."

Rey took his hand and clasped it with both hands.

"I can't stay too long. I just came to tell you that Sophie is not doing too well. She has stage 4 breast cancer. She'll be gone in less than 24 hours."

"That's terrible. We stayed in touch over the years."

"She had a good life. She saw all her children grow up and get married and she was able to have time with her grandchildren."

Jack's eyes began to well up.

"I went to see her also," Rey shared.

"You did?" Jack's voice responded with a robust tone. "Does she still have the sweater you knitted for her?"

"She does. She wants to be buried wearing it."

"I saved that little piece of paper that you wrote to me at the end. And the rosary. I carried them with me all these years."

Rey looked at him lovingly.

"You saved Sophie."

Jack started to cry and he could barely form words between the tears.

"No. You saved her. And you saved me."

Rey bent down, hugged Jack, and kissed him on the cheek. He reciprocated and felt at peace.

"Soon," Rey disclosed, "you'll be in a place where no one dies and no one cries."

"Can I go with you now?" Jack pleaded.

"Not now. Soon."

"Can you stay with me for a while?" Jack begged.

"I can't. There are other Jack's and other Sophie's out there who need me. Don't worry about anything."

Rey gave Jack a final hug and kiss on the cheek.

"Goodbye, Jack."

"Goodbye, Rey."

Rey turned and left the room. Jack looked out the window and closed his glass cover. He thought about his life and in particular, an adventure that had occurred forty-one years earlier, over a three-day period, with the Queen of Heaven.

The next morning at approximately 7:00 am, Jack's heart stopped beating. It was said that he had a smile on his face.

Outside of his window, the sun radiated brightly on Carlsbad and the people of Southern California. For those who believe, the sun was just a little warmer.

About the Author

Vince Aiello grew up in upstate New York before moving to Southern California where he attended California Western School of Law. He is admitted to practice law in both New York and California. *3 Days till Dawn* is his sixth novel and his second faith-based action thriller. His first faith-based action thriller was the bestseller, *Faith Full*. His earlier legal thriller novels, *Legal Detriment*, *The Litigation Guy*, *Legion's Lawyers,* and *Lethal Equity* were all acclaimed bestsellers. Visit his website at www.vinceaiello.com.

<u>ACKNOWLEDGEMENTS</u>

I would like to thank the following individuals for providing support and inspiration for *3 Days till Dawn*:

Ethan P. Aiello
Sarah Rose Aiello
Valerie R. Aiello, RPh
Lucila Anibarro
Nina Eiffert
Beth Jurecki
Mark Jurecki
Rev. William Marquis
Rev. Michael Robinson

www.ingramcontent.com/pod-product-compliance
Lightning Source LLC
Chambersburg PA
CBHW071549040426
42452CB00008B/1118